D1194643

New and Selected Poems: 1942-1997

John Tagliabue

New and Selected Poems: 1942-1997

John Tagliabue

ACKNOWLEDGMENTS

Some of the poems in this collection are drawn from five previous volumes:

Poems (New York: Harper, 1959)
A Japanese Journal (San Francisco: Kayak, 1966)
The Buddha Uproar (San Francisco: Kayak, 1970)
The Doorless Door (New York: Grossman, 1970)
The Great Day (Plainfield: Alembic, 1984)

The author thanks also the editors of the journals and anthologies in which many of the poems have appeared: *Am Here Forum, Andover Review, Apple, Before the Rapture, Big Moon, Bitterroot, Blue Buildings, Boston Rev., Bridge, Burning Water, Carolina Quarterly, Centennial Rev., Central Park, Chants, Chariton Rev., Chelsea Rev., Cold Mountain Rev., Compass Rose, Contemporary New England Poetry, Ct. Register Citizen, Dallas Rev., Dust, Elf, Embers, Endless Mountains Rev., Epoch, Epos, Fiddlehead, Fire in the Sea, Foxtail, Galley Sail Rev., Garnet, Genesis, Georgetown Rev., Great River Rev., Greenfield Rev., Green Mountains Rev., G.W. Rev., Hudson Rev., Hummingbird, Icarus, Images, Kayak, Kennebec, Kestrel, Kosmos, Live Poets Society, Longhouse, Maine Times, Main St. Rag, Margin, Massachusetts Rev., Mostly Maine, Nedge, New Letters, New Virginia Rev., New York Quarterly, North Atlantic Rev., Northeast, Northern New England Rev., Oxford Magazine, Penumbra, Pacific International, Poetry* (Chicago), *Poetry East, Poetry Northwest, Poetry Now, Poets On, Practices of the Wind, Prairie Schooner, Puckerbrush Rev., Pulpsmith, Redstart, Sante Fe Sun, Shaman, Slow Dancer, Smith, South Florida Poetry Journal, Spring, Stonecloud, Stone Country, Texas Quarterly, Undine, Via, Vision, Voices International, West Coast Rev.,* and *Wordplay.*

Published by The National Poetry Foundation
University of Maine, Orono, Maine 04469-5752

Printed by Cushing-Malloy, Inc.
Ann Arbor, Michigan 48107

Distributed by University Press of New England
Hanover and London

The National Poetry Foundation
University of Maine
Orono, Maine 04469-5752

Library of Congress Number: 97-67208
ISBN 0-943373-44-1 (cloth)
ISBN 0-943373-45-x (paper)

CONTENTS

Dedicated to Grace, Juniper, Tera, Phoebe, Alexander

Poems (1942-1958)

He walks in a fine fire of atoms
So continual, like light about his head,
That he has never dreamed of cold or storm,
Or nakedness disgusted with itself, or envy
Poisoning used arrows to be shot again,
This time to reach and kill.

He walks in the first mist, the one
Before creation rested. He is affection
Not yet distilled, distinct; incapable of dying.
His thoughts are kisses, fecund as the weightless
Waters of the deep love turned that day to spray;
And still they dance in him.

THE SEA GULLS IN THEIR SPLENDOR

The sea gulls in their splendor bow and kiss the whirling air
    and dive and die
And find in foam the risen spring and bring the fish as
    bird or word
And dive and die into the sun and bring the son to glory
    in the sky
And dive and die in lover's breast and bring the sun to rest
    in the cool night.

THOSE ABYSSES OF SILENCE

Those abysses of silence where roses grow, where women
    out of the foam comb their hair,
Where lions in the golden lair sleeping by the sun at
    night high in the mountains
Walk like saints over the seas of air, there on such
    majesties of thoughts,
The dreamers looked down and looked above and realized
    in the moment and forever
That they were the children of God. Out of his side came
    Eden and out of beauty
Shone the moon and the lions and lambs and birds and
    snakes and stones
Quietly conceived in their dream. And the stillness of
    Eve grew warm
And the dawn came to their desire as they saw God as
    Sun or bird in a celestial tree.

THE SEA GULLS

These lovers have wandered away from each other into the shadows
    of their forgetting, the sea gulls brighten,
The purest white of purest love, all celebrating the
    Sundays of doves,
Breaking now over their memory as grass over the graves of the dead,
Then swoops the white winged wide winged angel or bird,

radiant sea gull,
He from Christ, and into the sea touches gently once more
    with his desire,
The Sun's necessary ever necessary love, and the lovers find each other's
    way again on the blowing blowing sands,
But finally great day, their blessed sea salty arms embrace
And the white silent thunder of sea birds speaks to their
    closed and wise eyes.

THE WAY TO BREATHE

1.

The way to breathe is to give away your life
To a poem or to a woman in the forest
All stars hide and all gods abide in each bird's cry
Or dying twig. They wait. Upon summer's roundness
In the night as a mother moon jewelled
With crickets and the art of insects the dancing of the unseen
We met we met it is in meeting that we know the divine
Was meant for us and that unity abides in the love of the
    universe.

2.

Quietly quietly quietly a thing is born the dawn comes
A flower is found on the way to the sea
A flower is found on the way from the sea
The sea is a flower your body waits for me
I see I see that all this green this sparkling of your body
Is green is sparkling I see in night or day milk or stars
Breasts of the day dreams of wide sleeping by a quiet sunny lake
Under coolest pines, the truth frightening growing,
Quietly quietly quietly I spoke my hope and life to you.
You answered too. I saw the children by the lakes of summer.

WHY IS THE FIRE SO WIDE

Why is the fire so wide in your breast, robin red breast ?
Why is the sky so passionate in your calm song as you delicately
     confront
The wide bright emotional day like a singer ? You carry the
     passions of the heavens
And if a forest fire were to burn it would be nothing compared to your
     flame and fame and flight. All night long I thought of
     God's fire
Of how gentle the song of passion, the red bush, the bright moment
Was when singer and song, bird and listener, God and word, were one.
All is won in your beauty and flight. The red feathers overwhelm the
     giddy rolling world. The word is on fire.
Receive this apparent sunset and God is always arisen.

LOOKING AT A TREE

Looking at a tree, a young tree too, I remembered all my ancestors.
I was out hunting that day. What I was hunting for I don't know,
Maybe poems, maybe a girl, maybe a Persian rug. Anyway words
Came to me as I looked at the tree and saw the heads of various families,
Some like animals, some mythological, some like maidens in a Persian
     manuscript,
Some like lovers too close to mention their names. I was standing still
     and wondering
When I felt so happy that I did not struggle to say anything.
I would say that something was successful.

THE WORLD LEAPING AND TURNING
AS TWO LOVERS SIT IN BED AND TALK

A dream becomes a body
As the sea becomes a fish
As a rising lover
Becomes father and star.

A dream becomes a woman
A dream becomes a wife
A dream becomes a husband
As universal life.

They sat in bed and spoke
They rolled in the wheel of stars
Their children sang around them
Like the fish in the leaping sea.

THE MOON HELPS GIVE BIRTH TO THE CHILD

The moon that pulls the tide of our eyes, our yearning for Mary and
    God,
That pulls the Milky Way, the moons of her dream, and makes her sing
    as she sleeps,
Now calls the sleeping and waking child with his kingdom of crowns
    and dreams
Around his soft and startling hair and the sleepy kingdom of the loins.
Pearls are made. Galaxies are said. Lovers are married. Birds in the dark
    watch
And spread their wings towards the galaxy as the new born child finds
    the breast
And sings to his mother about Mother and God.

TO BE DAZED

To be dazed that is the way of all messengers of the sun,
I saw a robin sit on three low heavens, three blue eggs,
And absolutely still thinking of eternity know creation was coming
Into time out of the three blue heavens to ask for love, to sing,
She knew the God who made her forever mother and world and
    stillness,
And then flew, flew, knew, that the time had come for time
In its feathers and its glory to return God's story by flying and singing,
We were all, including Creation, amazed.

THE INSTINCTS OF INSECTS

1.

A leaf sails like a boat, so does a word so does a world so does a tear,
Why in this summer set of insects of butterflies and weeds by singing
    water
Clear as God, why does a woman cry, a lover die?
An insect folds its wings in green there to be seen
By Death's Sun for a moment, on that stream,
Through that dream, what port does it seem,
What port does it seem we are reaching ?
The arms of the angels are like the sun light.

2.

In their green excitement the darning needles unfold their wings,
The Japanese dancers have learned their art from them,
Unfurl their colored secrets as the lanterns of a festival
Startle young lovers and as butterflies amaze the world,
In and out between the weeds between mornings and out of evenings
The fireflies or lovers or poets with lanterns walk.
Here is a quiet place to talk where insects are singing.

3.

The lady bug in her shell of beauty
Speaks of the grandeur of God
Of the varied colors and love of the cosmos
In her small darkness she contains all secrets
In her walking all poems.
As she goes in circles she bewilders us with her theology and destiny
And as she flies away we write a poem.

4.

The sacred mother beetle makes a home for her unborn child
As round as the universe or the universal word and in this miracle
The child grows and goes slowly from chamber of food and knowledge
To chamber of food and knowledge where he will have to be a
    sacred king.
The sudden shock startles him into color and as he speaks
For a moment poems and God bow to this celebrating instinct.

5.

To renounce the world is perhaps to gain a poem or a saint, to announce
the world is perhaps to gain a garden or a woman,
To renounce the self is perhaps to gain a universe, to announce the
universe is perhaps to gain a self,
The beetle that saw its lover knew the universe was meant for him
and the universe that saw the beetle
Knew that love was meant for you.

6.

The light pleasure of darning needles chasing each other, can a poem
equal that ?
The Sun as Emperor must be dazed, must have dozed into one or
two of these
In jealousy of splendor and joy, over the stream they whirl in
undescribable ecstasy
Making gods and words seem ponderous, they whirl
And settle in the thin green weeds to be with the coolness and
excitement
Of the Sun's words.

7.

Dazed and amazed the poet learned the alphabet of midnight love
From the firefly and he began to fly about the shore and told a tale
Of kings who out of their sides brought forth palm trees and women.
The women in the shades by boats, their breasts like summer, the
fishermen
Forgot their trade and pulled up God all wet and glowing from the
amorous sea.

A SUMMER POEM

Certainly I am related to you bird
you with the flame sitting calmly surrounded by the paradise of
the day
I know your readiness to flight
And your heart's need.
Near me a small bird hopped into a dark growing tree a bush
with God
And then it flew away into the day I did not at the moment see.

I wrote the poem. Bird, if you come into the room
    into the paper
Who will die and how shall we fly into what paradise ?
The mysteries of ecstasy are everlasting. I saw the day
    where I had seen the bird.

THE CAROUSEL IN THE TUILERIES

The children go up and down on the merry go round
What a sound. The trees are all around
Like light and shade how still they stand
As if no other day but this existed.
It begins again, slowly they move
Like waking up our head goes round
And then a little faster. The trees still
Are gorgeous as the gods within the woods
The blue balloon is rising as the joy
And now they faster go like birds around the gods
The center is their dream, our hope, our love,
They whirl now through the sea.

And softly it comes back upon the earth
Slowly it turns. The perfect girl in blue
Looks at the gods all pleased and then it stops.

WINTER and SPRING
A ceremony-and-song

1.
Fears freeze as ice
the meadow brook
the wordless winter day
—No Skating Please—
—no children's play

—for underneath's the heart!

2.
The hills roll and are
empty. Pregnant of space
and what's between.
Tall grasses sweep the horizon.

What's to be feared in emptiness,
the valley of rolling hills,
what's between life and life ?

3.
The round hills,
low and round and warm,
swell the bell
of truth and love
which rests within
the hands of feeling;

the sight of round hills,
dappled cows, short grass,
brown fields, brown trees,
rings the wild bell
and feelings are as
joyous as the sound.

4.
She came in lilies like the spring,
Wet and white,
To bring the dew to wash my brow,
Kind and light,
To bring the fragrance of the morn,
Cool and bright,
To tempt the hand to touch,
To win, to hold, to love, to live,
Fierce and bright.
She came in lilies like the spring
To love, to live, to dance, to sing.

5.
So I know that spring is here
and with new sweep the wind
between the trees of winter's
wail for cool is grass

and naked is my will
I sing and sit upon the
grass and welcome spring.

6.
Rank riots
Rule the spirit;
Outward and inward they clash,
The fight of sounds and armor
On the mind. Rule riots,
Reason, rings the chapel
Preacher, but springtime
Breaks his bones; and life
Is growing wild as new
Born grass.

7.
The black-eyed suzie sits upon the grass
bemoans its fate to a glass
sky; (why so high today tonight ?)
one black eye is silent cast
as a pirate at the mast
upon a sullen today tonight
sky: (why so low and sad ?)

it moved its head and bees began
to make a laurel buzz
of light (a black ring buzz)
about self-sorrow seeking own
delight: (why so low, why so high ?)
why is love so far apart ?

8.
So many places am I in I,
me and presence where is it;
the changing seasons and
geography within the soul
and all is navigating strange
ly light and lyrical
is all the way from here
to Africa and back, it is
it is my wings of what
and that and longing o

so longing that I fly:
China's here and there's
a Jersey cow and violets
from Italy and Spain.

9.
Unseen violets,
only known
by ten toes,
why must die ? why must die ?
before my eyes
before these hands could have you ?
Why must die, unseen clover,
unseen violets, why must die ?
Hark ! from the dead
there's no answer;
if there were, if there were,
there would be
Seen Unseens,
live-dead clovers,
a revealed philosophy.

10.
Like a pearl, like a row of pearls, on a fiery wheel
Each sacred word, angel, turned the world
And man's dream awoke and proclaimed the Truth.

11.
Deep as the beard of a sage
High as the waving of a tree
Unseen as the voyage of a bird
Mighty as the song of the sun
Married as Man and Woman
Blessed as Man and Woman
Is every Creative Act.

12.
Take this hand. The tree reached out.
Take this foot. The ground was courteous.
Take this thought. The sky was abundant.
Take this love. The child was glorious.

Take this moment. The world was momentous.
Take this universe. The bride was starry.
Take this Christ. The Easter was full of joyous lambs.
Take this God. I was everywhere in sleep, creation and joy.

THE BARE ARMS OF TREES

Sometimes when I see the bare arms of trees in the evening
I think of men who have died without love,
Of desolation and space between branch and branch,
I think of immovable whiteness and lean coldness and fear
And the terrible longing between people stretched apart as these
        branches
And the cold space between.
I think of the vastness and courage between this step and that step
Of the yearning and fear of the meeting, of the terrible desire
        held apart.
I think of the ocean of longing that moves between land and land
And between people, the space and ocean.
The bare arms of the trees are immovable, without the play of leaves,
        without the sound of wind;
I think of the unseen love and the unknown thoughts that exist
        between tree and tree
As I pass these things in the evening, as I walk.

THERE ARE SO MANY PEOPLE

There are so many people
That am I,
So many voices confuse me.
That I must find a darkness
Where I can play my record back,
Meet Hamlet and Christ
Without my presence.
But I am too much with me,
And I must find a darkness
Which is Fullness too;
So I will meet my soul

And not my photograph.
I shall meet myself,
Clasp hands,
But know that I am dead.

CAST OUT, CAST OUT

Cast out, Cast out, the talking word,
A beggar dies for it;
Upon an empty street walks he
With hurt and wounded feet.
Now follow now, Now follow him,
He may but need a word.
Is he your brother or your son?
(Or are you really he?)

I bring some water for his wound,
He looks and pities mine;
The joy begins to stir his feet,
The water turns to wine.

THE PHILOSOPHERS IN THE FORESTS

He who writes with stones and brooks and nooks and lovers
With stones in brooks, birds on the twig, stars on the clear night,
White light in the winter sky, writes with eternity; there are no secrets
Only many lives in which each word will be a talking life
Or talking stone or tree who is an actor and whose rhetoric
Makes this stage a growing knowledge. All is here, now and forever, ·
Though we ever go like priests or rabbits, children or the dying,
Lovers or hermits through the forests of God.

THE RAINBOW BROUGHT A ROSE TO ME

The rainbow brought a rose to me
And held it in my palm.
O lamb, why do I see
The blood and still no harm?

The blood and still no harm
My love, the chaste and still the free,
Why must I see the rose, my love,
Instead of seeing thee?

I love the passion of the rose,
I even cry for it,
But for the passion of your hand,
O, I would die for it.

The blood is on the rose, my love,
For you are dead I see,
And tears that come from out my heart
Are of my blood for thee.

FOR TO CONQUER EXCELSIS FLOWER

For to conquer Excelsis Flower
Singing O Chorus of Angels and
Breaking O Roses of God. For
To conquer Flesh and Blood
Is Praise and Royal Battle;
O shout the breaking of the
Mystic Rose. Flesh and Blood
Is Contemplation. And From the Rose
Six Angels Trident-tongued are Born,
And my poor ears are Broken
And my poor Flesh is Cast Away
And in this Contemplation, the Holy
Mouth of Rose, I perish now, O God,

I perish now with joy, O God.

Piero,
    peer and prince,
        seer and scientist
        of love. The blue sky of your clear truth
Dazes my memory still and fills its skies with love.
I see the great pure horses and the still warriors dazed by the day
When Christ clearly dawned on them and the thin trees of spring sing.
I see the women of the fair civilization waiting and speaking softly.
The music in the court, the music in the cubism of your thought,
Amazes us still as armies pursue the truth. And I see behind the altar
In the church of St. Francis in Arezzo also blessed by clarity and
    the blue air
A sick man pure and holy as a lamb being resurrected by the
    cross of truth.

THE BEAUTIFUL HOUSE

beautiful house are you going to sleep
are you closing your shutters? will your plants be quiet?
will the boards stay in their places and not go to visit friends?
and besides that will the sun and the stars and the mouse stay outside?
I once saw a house that had so many friends it was hardly ever at home
and once I saw a home in a poem like a snail but when I saw the stars
talking to the house that night and she was silent I knew she
would stay where she was.

TARQUINIA

When I think of some readers reading me whose names I do not know
    and they are far away
(Though in ways I know them better than the letters of the alphabet and
    they are very near)
I think of sheep standing as I saw them once by the radiance of wheat
    and the soft glow of the sea
In Tarquinia over the old mounds of happy Etruscan tombs, I remember
    going into these cool tombs with my wife

And seeing the freshness of the paint, the delight of the painter, the
    dancers in delicate knowledge
Approaching, and so the reader and the writer approach each other
    carrying gifts
That make death a light festival. I think too of lovers asleep who have
    dreamt us both into existence.

THOUGHTS AND SONGS OF A YOUNG MAN ASLEEP BETWEEN SPRING AND SUMMER

1.
The daughter of the well keeper's water
was a cool young miss who could kiss
most strangely casually who could keep water cress
near her breast and in the summer when the waves turned up
she could show you birds flying in the field
or fish swimming in the stream by brown weeds
and exotic songs that no one but one so deep and cool
could know. Don't hesitate, fool, go.

2.
It is better not to say so much and row
and if the sunset betrays you sleep in jade
for a hard century but like a duck breaking its
beak through winter air through winter wail
you will rise never mind princes
but like what is better than nature
a joyous victorious man, good, in love.

3.
If on a certain day you dig sand
and find a golden grain
do not be startled if it grows
before your eyes
into God.

4.
If a rose is closed
and a secret desires to open

the rose wet will open
and an older secret will be born.

5.
The night may not be counted in stars
nor in the animals that prowl the galaxies
but in agonies, agonies. The love cannot be counted
in moons in moons that slice through the night
but in you but in you. I am falling asleep
I am climbing a tree who are you there to take me
beyond the physical tree into the sky?

GOOD FRIDAY IN PROCIDA

A boat
with my family
sailed before the dawn came
and it was still very dark and cold
to a small island near Ischia,
an island where there was a large Penitentiary
on a hill, and the beautiful sea and sky everywhere,
where this day, Good Friday, many people in black
remembered and re-enacted as still partly in the Dream
The Passion of the Lord, the Fisherman, the Sun.
They and we and maybe He walked past small stores
selling Easter bread and large lemons, past small dark eyes and caves,
walked slowly up as the dawn began to join us in our walking
the mysterious hill of the small colorful quiet radiant town
surrounded by the infinite and delicate beauty of the sea
now growing lighter even as the Child was radiant at his birth
and our always death. We went up partly as in a dream
the narrow winding ways by crowds of people part of the Passion
in black, the little houses in a dim and radiant pink or blue
or violet or yellow or white. We waited until the sound of death
as a cry from the bottom of roots or from a dead child or from a wound
of Christ entered the flower of the dawn and three eternal musicians
with instruments more primitive than man sounded the deep
sound of sorrow. It tore our hand. And then the procession began
and when and where it began and ended we do not know because
it is a play and a community of watchers and waiters and sufferers
and parents and children and bakers and butchers and priests and

prisoners
forever part of the waking heart since Adam carried the invisible tree
out of Eden and the cold sky wept like the flesh of Eve. The
beauty of man and woman there in the gray and shocking dawn of
our murder, though we are the murdered one too; the keeper of the
    prisoner is not known
from the prisoner even as the sky is not known from our hand
now invisibly bleeding as the priests and the partakers and children
in the white of His Death walk unceremoniously down the winding way
to enter the Tomb of the Church. Voices like fish
    or flowers or stones
were part of the sound of the day as in distance from above unseen
the Body of the Lord was approaching us. Women wept. And the bodies
    of lambs
tied to a cross, the bodies of doves made into a cross, the children in
    white
carrying crosses on their backs, many children in white carrying the
    banquets of the Last Supper
with fish with flowers for eyes, and petals over their sparkling sea
    rainbows went past us.
Mothers remembered the dying of their husbands and sons and for
    hours the signs of the cross,
the signs of agony like the parts of Mankind
were separated and carried before us as food is broken as the Sun goes
    dry hanging on the Tree.
And then the Body of Christ like a quiet and ever present burst of flames
or birds in loss of migration in the body of our bleeding and lostness
summoned themselves to our vision and the eyes and doors and hands of
    the Church;
and the heavy music played beyond all its funeral march coming to us
    like Tragedy
and we saw made of the Tree made of Man Christ with his wounds
as we died on the street and the mothers and children and shadows
of the dead like the leaves entering the ground followed the triumphant
    body
into the resurrection of the invisible Church, the invisible sea, the
    invisible Sky, the ever visible wonder of You.

THE ISCHIA PROSE-POEM

1.

A YOUNG BOY BY THE GREEN SEA

I was born by the sea, born on the sea maybe, there I found myself, by the sands a young boy playing, listening, watching, I collected sea shells, the green ripples of the sea rushed to me always telling my soul some story which in my love or joy my soul always repeats, rocked on the sea by the moon. But in the day I squatted on the sand and watched and listened and the wind was a joy. It was a companion for me. And we rushed over rocks together. I saw from the beginning of time fishermen putting out their nets, fishing boats at night traveling with lights like moving stars. The sea itself in my dreams was a friend. I ran with my dog. I watched them clean the fish, bait the hooks, repair the sea-worn brown-red nets, the tangle of divinity, I watched them slowly walk as in a dream by mountain and sea, supervised by sun and moon and all the turning romantic tunes of my childhood dreams and pleasures. I walked into the clear cold, sometimes even warm, water, my bare feet feeling the pebbles. I touched them. Messages were sent all over. My body swam. I loved it, my body, the sun, the water, the splashing, the coolness. Sometimes I saw groups of small fish swimming by me, dispersed by my larger presence like a planet. I liked to look at the night, both in summer and winter, it had a story for me, the stars I knew were divine. I loved them.

I also enjoyed drying in the sun. The wet water rolled from me, I was cool and dreamy. I loved myself. I also loved what I saw. The people were good. Though I cried often expecting things I think I did not get, expecting what was yet to come, what is yet to come. I found sea shells, all kinds like many poems. I loved them too though I knew people would think I was silly. I realized that they were a mystery and that their having achieved a beauty, a completion, after being under the sea and time was what made them divine secrets, indications of the gods.

I played in the sun. I ran I was happy.
Often I cried, but it was because I expected what it was not yet time for me to have and still do though many things have happened. More is to come as this sea is infinite. I looked over its blue and green. I watched, many days sometimes in slowness sometimes in absolute stupor some-times in happy stillness I watched and saw the fishermen and boats coming to and fro, the fish caught, unloaded, thousands of them at a time, sold. I saw that I would be a man, that I could do that; also I saw it must have been at the same time Christ blessing the sea and all fishermen.

2.

THE DEATH OF HIS FATHER

We sat by his coffin which was like a boat, I mean his bed for he was not dead yet. The doctor said he would die soon and left the room. We knew this too by the faraway look in his eye and also the last breath of his flesh as it were, the last hopeless clutch of anguish. He held on to the line tying him to the shore. But we knew and he felt in a way that is more shocking than knowledge the boat was breaking away. We were calm and almost still in the diurnal routine and in the poor dark room. But all around us was a storm like wild animals chasing at our hearts or a wild wind or turmoil, it beat around the room, or like sharks in the sea eating at the body of a child. All this hate swirled silently around us, the devils trying to take our souls away. He was afraid too for he knew as everyone in the room around his coffin-bed knew the great weakness and tearfulness of man, the hate that in our fear or weakness we can be possessed with. Over his bed was a crucifix. One of the devils took it into his hands obscenely and played with it swinging it over our heads. We were confused, we were almost lost and our whole life's struggle would have been meaningless and lost; but a greater cross as a voice of my father, as an arm and hope of my father swung over all things, a great large shadow over our heads, it swung, my father looked at us through the great distance of suffering which he had been through, came closer to us and almost smiled, we knew he knew our sins as he had known his own, he knew, and he loved us. O how he loved us ! so that all the devils crept away hurriedly or flew out of the window in a blind eternal defeat. We looked at him, held on to the line, I loved him, I gave him a kiss; the line broke and the boat sank suddenly distantly into the night. But I saw his eyes forgiving us for he was one of us and I saw his beautiful eyes blessing us and knowing that though division was difficult re-union and re-birth would be as sure as when one summer night he rowed strongly joyously back to us on shore with many fish in his net and both of us together had many stars in our mind and in our love. We greeted him so easily.

3.

A FISHERMAN ON CHRISTMAS EVE

The sea is dark and cold, I don't see a star. I don't see a cloud. Just cold dark water, tons of water, beyond me, I am floating on a wooden stick in this night. The cold breezes blow. The fish must be far below, far away. Yet I do not wish I were home in bed. This cold night means something to me like a prayer, like a cold monk's cell where there is nothing there. And waiting and rowing. I love my lovely wife. After this long and necessary night is over I will go to her and as if in a dream enter her dark bed room and we will lie warmly under the bed sheets and know that stars circle our world.

Our two heads will be together and our bodies will be very warm and happy next to each other. That is there on the shore like those small houses, children of our dream. They wait and palpitate. They look out and fear and wonder and pray and are warm. They wait. They gather darkness for our happiness. She waits in bed for me. Her eyes are out and hunt around the room like stars. She startles. She almost sits up knowing that outside those walls I am thinking of the beauty and the love and pleasure she can sweetly warmly give. Her waiting blesses my sailing. I sail out. Darkness I am not afraid of you. You are like a cold coat that makes me know inside of me is God, inside the sea are flashing fish, inside my lovely house is my wife. Here, I'll let down this lamp, this basket, this word, this temptation of a lobster net and the red lobster will be caught. I'll present one to the Virgin. For even when there are no stars or moon my mother like the unseen moon blesses me and tells these seas what songs to sing and somehow tells the fish where they should go. And my father too like an image in a church that frightens me yet made me to admire as a boy, a saint that gathers night and stars into himself, is here right here very near enormous as a figure in this atmosphere of coldness night and sea. He follows me and we have loved. He blesses me. I bless the fish I catch. The lobster like a mind searching eternity or a lover his love crawls into the trap of time. The child is in the womb. The Christ is in the world. Now I see the star. O gentle ship, O lovely blessed ship, now we will go home and wish my wife Merry Christmas.

TEN RELATED POEMS*

1.
a woodpecker without his bride pecks
                         tap   tap   tap
and so I without you type
                         love   love   love
I always see you in a tree
                         or in a sky
the skies came to us one day and learned about children
                birds from the South
returned speaking of Christ and flowers surprising after the snow
                woke our children up
under the sun the memory of you created universes.

* (These poems were written while thinking of (1) my wife who was away for a few days (2) my sister (3) my wife (4) my mother and her father (5) my father (6) myself at the typewriter (7) my father's mother (8) my mother's mother (9) my father's gruff father (10) my daughters, Francesca and Diana.)

2.
she in her darkness burned

first a very distant flower
then a very nearby darkness growing larger
and then being born

there was something old and wise about her childhood
and her large eyes showed a knowledge of tragedy-and-man she never
        could speak
she was even then, twelve years old with lovely breasts, a spanish dancer
and she could never speak about the life she knew like the whirling and
        distant fire of all the galaxies
for a moment I danced with her
and then like an arab tent she went away into a mystic country
but wherever I see fire of any kind I love her.

3.
O blissful bush
dark gauguin expanses
o watery place
I think of you high in the mountains of anywhere
but guatemala for instance
squatting making pots and gods
under weavings of heavy rainbows startling all the elements of the air
and my desire like sleepy indians in narrow streets in flowered lanes
in perfumed shadows dozing remembering the ancient gods of
stone and of Sun

        you took them all back under your darkness
and in several centuries of writing you filled the higher civilizations of
        upper guatemala with loveliness
I think of you when I see those lakes close to the skies and birds of sun
        and gods
when I see the water and divinity.

4.
parsley
        mother
rice
        sarcastic half-wit
you made me smile and cry
like a baby
like a god in love with the sun

you were always cooling me so I would not have to leave this world
you with my father made me out of God
as God made you out of God and my grandparents too
I will always remember your silly and ancient and shiftless and sweet
father taking me through the chestnut woods
and taking me without purpose it seemed then to summer hills to see
      friends of his
and once when I arrived very late at night in Italy sleepy giving me a
      bowl of milk and bread
now I see the divine purpose as he is no longer in his grave
and as you are chanting nonsense in your inner core's sweetness
pretending you are stingy and sarcastic.

I see your lovely heart is like the green field of creation.

5.
father
      Father
           God
swamp
    fire
         darkness
         everywhere of beginning
I cannot say your name
      hippopotamus god
they say you had a mistress all your life
      but she is nowhere to be seen in my poems
      so I will leave her out of this
she must have been nothing to distract you like the
      American civilization of cement that also
      meant absolutely nothing to you
so that you could really darkness and fire and absolutely speech-
      less philosopher and mysterious priest
      that you really are
concentrate on God and without what the frivolous and secular
      call thought give love to everyone.
I thank you.

6.
all I have to say about myself for the moment, dear Reader, is
    I speak
    I type
    I love you

7.
grandmother
>how many children did you have
>11, 13, 16, all the children of the world?
>it doesn't really matter
>to me
>or from where you are.
But every one of your eleven handsome strong magnificent fierce
>some mystical
>all amorous
>some who threw a general off a cliff in the first
>world war
sons (or suns)
say you were great.
>My father who does not waste words and who is
>never reasonable says you are God.
I saw you on the farm
>with a shawl and making polenta.
They all say you are God.
>When we all see each other again I know we will
>know it is true. But you will say the same thing
>to us.

8.
you took me to church
we climbed up a curving stone way on a lovely Sunday
I proud even of your shadow
and you blessed me with a few mumblings
and the great church swung like the censer of a celestial boy
and your feet were as they are now in heaven
the incense and the darkness held me around Christ and now I
>remember.
O the holiness of walking with you ! bleeding and resurrected one !
Why are so many birds carrying us ?
In the darkness at night you told me stories by the fire too.
O I see that we are both swinging in that celestial censer above a poem.

9.
Gruff
>and Gruff
>>and guff
old Lombard Grandfather pitching hay and seeds and suns
why were you there by the hay and horses and green suns sprouting
>from the fresh and dewy blades of grass

pretending old mumbling and gruff old patriarch to scare me ?
O I see your laughter now like the horses and the pitching hay and your
        flying suns.
Go ahead and scare me, lovely God. You are making more children.

10.
I have two lovely daughters too
and will be silent
after such a sunny day of writing and remembering
to hear their song
and see them grow.
O Dear Reader, see how you are growing !!

IN THE NAME

    In the name of the Father
        and the Son
        and the Holy Ghost
        in a grain of rice.
We believe in purity and God's ever Sunday Splendor
        Day of the Sun
        voice of the Lamb
        abundance of rice.
We believe in the white bride by the side of the moon
        and the dark husband by the side of the fountain
        and the green mountain by dreaming priests
        and the fragrance of the rice.
We believe in the marriage celebrated forever in the white ceremony
        of the rice and the rice fields where poets wade
        and the night where stars supervise dancers
        and when lovers sleep dreaming of Creation.

THE WIDE EXPANSE OF THE ROOTS OF A GREAT TREE RIPPED OUT OF THE EARTH BY THE HURRICANE, ITS CAPILLARIES SHOWING LIKE MANY HISTORIES AND MEMORIES

The great tree fallen, its gentle roots a magnificence,
A map quietly exposed to the sky, a large world,
The grandfather torn asunder as he was blessing the sky with
    summer knowledge.
Where did the squirrels go, those priests ? The storm like darkness and
    man's sin
Self-hate broke through the holy bone and dust's map
Lies quietly, the wind like an insane dancer in the leaves
Ate like a witch and ghost all night. There was no bleeding.
Christ's blood grew stronger. And the holy night of the turning world
Full of death moan returned to its musical mystery beyond our bones
    and stars.

THE MASSACRE OF THE INNOCENTS

As the lights go on and off in the eyes of the living and dead
And the streets are crowded with boxes and people
The snow falls. The children are turned on and off.
The television tells us to buy this now
Whatever it is we do not know but it is impressed upon the tired nerve.
In the streets the cars wait like the dead.
The lights in the stores do not record our dream.
The people are crying as they search for the Child.

A WINTER

I by the washline watch the birds
    that from the frozen winter's finger tips have come
now to sit on spring and tell of Christ their Sun
who from their wings flew toward the window sill and still I see
his eyes right in the sky

and then the beggars in the snow did ask for crumbs
and I all warm with song remembering a winter in my bone
threw them my self

and from that day on the sky has not undone us.

IF DEATH WERE NOT A BEGINNING

If death were not a beginning
Then life would be an end
And the cattails and the tall grass
And the dew that hangs on lovers' eyes
Would all be monstrous and the grave
Would be a stillborn child.
But out of the night
As out of the mouth the poem
Comes a quite wild and howling child
Whose name was Christ
And blessed with the stars
He tells his thrice and million
And more than million glory
To any mother, lover, or listener.
Listen to resurrection sing.

The White Lamb in the Word is Still.

BY THE MARGIN OF THE WOOD

There by the margin of the wood, out of what history and lovely need,
    the bird alone sat calling to its mate
And the sky had answered before and after she in an unseen paradise of
    the lovely cool night
Answered with the frenzied song. The sky very wide answered them and
    they brought to it their flight
And the God each contained in the breast and song. They opened the
    sky for lovers that spring.
First they were unseen. The male opera singer I saw sitting on a twig the
    fire of his chest heaving

And then from a distant tree she sang and as they called out of the poems
    all lovers
The stars came gently and magnificently to our sky as I began to think of
    you before I wrote this poem.
They flew very near each other, paradise and you knew how near.
Do you hear the two of them singing under the heavy and beautiful stars ?

THEY GO

After the rain, the ants how they crawl having tried to move the world,
They return to their instinct and their freedom they go beyond woe,
Scampering by the grass the tall wonders of God, they know, they go,
Living and breathing and dying, each ant is itself a mountain and a sun
    and a rain cloud,
It carries marriage and death, it celebrates as it goes on its mission
    carrying existence,
The need to go beyond the world into the womb of eternity
Where all things seem to begin and end. But the priestly ant
Was silent about the mysteries. And the rain came again
Flooding the world with sorrow and the tears of Christ.

I SOUGHT ALL OVER THE WORLD

I sought all over the world for a present for you until I found the sky
And in it was the world and you and me. I was there with my love
    bright as the sun
You were there with your love moony as the night, dark, and pearls
    were everywhere for lovers,
The children climbed the trees on that bright and light day. I looked all
    over the world
For a present for you and then I made you see yourself and me in
    creation
In God and then I was, we were, very happy. The children laughed in
    the tree.

IN THE MORNING WHEN

In the morning when I see her naked like cyclamen or cycles of song
I am dazed and awakened like a horse dreaming going through dew
By streams of fresh dawn, the moss kissed, the insects making Japanese
    poems,
I rode on the light watching her wash herself, uplift her arm
As the dawn uplifts most poems. And roaming through the day
I cannot forget the way her breasts and awakening were part of the dawn
and my hope.

ONE MORNING AS I CALMLY LOVE MY HOUSE

Three grapefruit in a large blue and green vase on an Indonesian
    tablecloth in a peaceful room in the morning in Maine
On the third floor of a wooden house surrounded by months of snow
    and clear poems, including my wife and children
And a blue rug we bought in Mexico, these three grapefruit are peaceful
    like Chinese kings talking things over.

THE ROBIN REDBREAST IN THE NEST

The sky descended and the flame ascended and the nest became
    Noah's ark
And the song descended as rain into the tree growing leafier
And the flame ascended in her song to her children sitting in the nest
And the nest was carried around the world on the father on the mother
On love and desire. The clouds were calm and white as lambs now
And the radiant green is Creation too and each blade of grass
Sings to the mother bird as her children learn to sing
And as the wide flying sky sings to them and you.

THE PELICAN TOO CAN BE
KING OF THE UNIVERSE

You have a hardness and a wildness and a mildness that lovers do as well
    as moon and milky sea
And seeing the sea gulls fly you remember a sea night and sailboats
That floated from this life to the next and you were heard in death's
    kingdom
And there is a complex lovely nest the eggs were born and from the
    King's hand
Were given to this world as the surf lectured to lovers
And out of the King's body came the new world as pure as a word
As secret and silent and as loud and blazing as the most ever present Sun.

AN UNSEEN DEER

An unseen deer through seen shadows leaps through my heart
A seen deer through unseen songs leaps through winter
And spring, the shadow on the cold dawn, the green beginning,
Ending, leaping, singing, all are in his luminosity.
The King quietly sees us, his eyes swift stars in the leaves,
Blesses us with his power, and then the forest hides him and sings.

DEEPER AND DEEPER ONE GOES INTO THE FOREST

Deeper and deeper one goes into the forest
The true self is not known and the keeper of the forest is not known
More and more I will fast and pray and forget the world
Remembering the worlds, seeing all the cosmic animals in the night,
Writing all the poems. It will be a prayer.
And when the forest disappears speech will become the cosmos.

The Buddha Uproar (1955-1969)
and The India Travel Journal (1981)

If short poems
    can be like specks of sun
        on the Deep Sea think
            of what brilliant voyages
                they can help you make.

THE PRAISE OF ASIA BEGUN

1.

Towards
which dream
are you
dreaming?
your head
like a flower
has many aspects,
like a stone
has many hours,
our joy like
showers gives rise
to more drums and art;
the many ways of making
love are as bright as
the aspects of stone or sun.

2.

When he was making love to her
he seemed to have three heads, he
did it seven times, she seemed to
have three beds. she did it
eleven times, they were mathematicians
later, now they were flowery
politicians; they were like blue
city scapes of silhouettes of melody
in the distance by the sea; he
felt a flower at the center of his chest
as she ate his heart; she dove
as a flying angel as the ribbons
or river of night flew around

their many arms; they were
prepared for flowery battle;
I want to add again He said.

3.

A Ceylonese dancer
as soft as water
as strong as wind
as beautiful as a
sinuous woman
as beautiful as a
flower in the dark
as golden as desire
and memory found
you praising it
the way a husband
raises a Ceremony.

4.

A celestial drummer
makes silence of his noise;
it begins to demand of you
celestial drumming and sleep.
Keep at it, chariot wheels,
dreamer, keep shaking your head,
the whole cosmic bed
is scattering milk and flowers.

5.

The Hindu stones
are manuals of miracles,
handy men or gods touch
the breast, the rest is
Indian mythology like
pleased elephants that
represent in colorful
procession many nights
of Making It. But any
stone is the beginning of
the whisper which says Love.

6.

"THIS SIDE REPRESENTS A BUDDHIST STUPA
ADORED BY FLYING DEITIES"

When they touched hands populations grew;
when they threw flower pots at each other
they became flying deities; when bees
sang by them they gathered some noise
for their enclosed dream; when they
threw frying pans at each other fish leapt
out and became dancing prophets; when
the prophets went to sleep the keys to the
enclosed dream were stolen by awakening lovers.

THE STAR IN THE SEED RESPONDS TO OUR
NEED. THE SUN IN THE SKY TELLS US WE
HAVE JUST BEGUN

When
you
find
a
star
in
a
well
you
have
been
welcomed
by
insight

"THE BORDER OF A MANDALA CONSISTS OF A
'BARRIER OF FIRE' WHICH AT ONCE PROHIBITS
ACCESS TO THE UNINITIATE AND SYMBOLIZES
THE METAPHYSICAL KNOWLEDGE THAT 'BURNS'
IGNORANCE" —MIRCEA ELIADE: *YOGA*.

The nighted king
the king on fire
the body of the dead man uprisen holding his Diamond
the song's point proceeding past rivers and songs
        and the bones of birds
        and the skulls of sea animals
        and the scriptures of procreation
        wet and fire
        darkness and light

through
into
beyond
within
the barrier of fire the bearded shaking ceremony of the legs,
        the rattling of legends
        the occurrence suddenly of gods
        each giving Its Name
        each touching the established body
        once and for all
recurring, changing the courses of rivers and seconds;
        a quiet painter
        remembers the labyrinth of colors,
        the conflagration
        of the festival, the flaring of nations,
        the fragrance of the New World's
        Flowers.

THEY SAID OM AND YOU'RE HOME

An
elephant
decorated
with

seasons   was
galaxies   greeted
carrying   by
an   dancers
anthology   with
of   flowers
poems   in
from   their
town   hands.
to
town

A RATTLE OF CONTRASTS

My almond tree is surrounded by bees,
my swaying arms are surrounded by poems,
your tongue is surrounded by playing darkness,
the flame is surrounded by buzzing dancers,
each person imitates a growing temple
as he sends forth gods night after night,
they are like spacemen or like deep sea divers
or they are like the shadows by our bodies.

HINDU DIRECTORY

1.
"UPA"—NEAR; "SHAD"—TO SIT

Let me be up
on the Upanishads,
let me sit at the feet of the mountain,
let me sit at the feet of the sky; there is a buddha
        head to every insect, instinct,
        plant, person;
be a singing student: Listen in; audit the authority
        of the winds: rig-vedas,
        ragas, Ganges; sit at
        the feet of Whitman.

2.

HIGHER GESTURES: "HIEROGLYPH"—WHICH MEANS
LITERALLY "A SACRED CARVING"

Carve this word out of a mountain
or make it a design in water, with a stick, or a leaf, or boat,
or take your Hindu hands and make messages in the air
and then do a handstand and proclaim with your feet
and then return to Aum and walk about a bit

and as you do this with a Muse
or a hurdy gurdy man or guru
or world provoking friend or tea
master remember your very body
is a sacred carving of the Day.

*

The lion mounts the lioness again
and the dancer is very dizzy and noisy,
several moons shake by her ears,
the god returns to the murmuring bush
country instinctively in the dark
and Stands Spouting; heavy insects
moving in the tangled grass give
hints concerning allegories to all drowsy sports.

WHO KEEPS THE RECORDS?

The small bird
in autumn with a somewhat green head
in a very huge tree like Hinduism
    goes from leaf to leaf
    like the soul of a
Voyager reading the Scriptures.

THE DIVINE DANCERS

1.

DEVI THE THIN AND SINUOUS DANCER

What is all this fingering about?
As leaves open on a tree as a kiss comes toward me
What is all this delicate wiggling about
As a snake goes through precious grass
As a dream goes through precious night
As the arms of a dark young river like a girl
Go about your swooning dance
In and out goes the river you are one
As Time and Eternity are danced into one
By the sinuous journey of the stars

O the black night will her dancing never stop?

2.

THE LORD OF FIRE

The Lord of Fire is jewelled
His eyes are crocodiles
That grow under green seas
Of desire and he mounts slowly
As snakes the delicious curled mouth of leaves.

3.

PARVATI

The sensuality of the stone
Is the desire of the bone
Is the yearning of the river night
For the moon and snake eternity

The stone begs for the sculptor
The sculptor begs for the god
The god begs for vegetation
The poem begs for contemplation.

4.

APSARAS

What infinite delicacies love knows
As when Apsaras holds her hands above her head
Like an opening lotus
Or by her thigh
Like a closing sigh
Or in the air like sparkling stars
What infinite desires she makes us know.

5.

THE DARK HEAD

The dark head
Bows upon the dark couch
The dark wind bows upon the dark flower
Out of the flower come seeds out of the flower
Comes juice out of the flower comes the stairway
Of desire out of the flower comes closing
Out of the flower comes deep sleep and knowledge
Out of the opening and closing the hunting and finding
Comes the unknown flower that we strive for
That some in most musical ways call God.

BARNACLE BILL THE MYSTIC

Knock at the door of the sea
Go down the well and ask a saint if it found It
Pray at the word of a seed

There by the pitching darkness forming itself into an OM
There by the ship's beak by its destined direction with
    OM as its Captain
There by the waves curling mist from which the dead voices
    speak in Chorus
There by the rising turning groaning darkness by the
    hand of Fate
    by the shells of snails
By the moaning of children by the bones of sea birds
    by the speckled stones

by the hymns of sea weed
Do you see His Face appearing and disappearing
       the Drowned One who
       beckons to you? who asks you
to transform the ocean into a church and to find him
       in a casket there
       like a strange sailor singing.

THE RETURNING BARNACLED ONE ANSWERS

"How many battleships have you sunk?"

"Seventeen. They are called—

> Cruelty
> Hatred
> War
> Repression
> Prejudice and ponderousness
> Painful and Soul Killing Propriety
> Nationalism
> Impersonality
> Conformity to Clichés
> Torture of Young and Old
> Neglect of Relatives
> Lack of honoring the Old Masters
> Lack of reverence for New Artists
> Lack of love for artifice and fable
> Hanging on Limp to Grave Thoughts
> Lack of Joking and familiar mysticism
> Lack of Crafts, lack of Rhythmic Impulse,
>   lack of Joyous Output."

INSISTENT HINDU AND OTHERWISE

The joys of sex are so saucy so sumptuous
       so both tangible and intangible
       so raucous though often quiet
       so undescribable yet alert

so cool and in fire and
    renewing, so concerned
with grasping yet ungraspable, so in our possession like
    our memories or stagings of the gods
    yet a form of non-possessive love
so unique and multiplying that tigers and gazelles are born from
    their shadows and murmurings
so subtle and cosmic and necessary that clouds and downpours
    and rivers are synonymous with them
    and amorous motion.

A PANTHEISTIC PAINTER OF SIGNS

He climbed upon the billboard like a monkey or like a
    god who was to
surprise himself and with his paint brush made letters of
    all colors and as he
was swashbuckling and as he whistled as he shook his head
    in obeisance to the planetary motions
and molecular messages the letters that he depicted grew
    taller and taller, they led an
almost independent life and he and the letters and this
    gave him enough energy to stand
on top of a flying letter and invent another language,
    this in turn predicted more
    epics, love lyrics, and
descriptions of all kinds. Some of the billboards, monkeys and
    gods disappeared but the spirit of
    literature was vital.

YOU CAN GO VERY FAR AT THAT

The 1st time I learned to spell elephant I was transported,
    the elephant thanked me,
I rode on him until I could spell India and Hindu and
    "do you love me?"
again the elephant answered yes and this time with a

chorus of tigers,
soon I was able to spell Blake and forests and the world
    increased in wonder,
I didn't want to stop riding, it was great to be up there
    and I was really dressed up
and there were festivals in every village that I entered.
    When I opened a book birds flew out
    or rabbits came out of a word.
Then I saw a procession of elephants and even the Buddha.

OM AND SHANTI

Riding a Hindu horse one went all over
    the Cosmos
it never stopped becoming as colorful as
    It Is
other people felt free to ride on this horse
    as all people and plants
and animals and planets felt free all
    the time and Eternity
to babble about God. I slept by the
    dream of Shiva
I awoke by the Dance of Karma. We
    all saw the Horse
feeding and sporting in the Cosmos and never
    can the languages of God
cease to be colorful since we were Singing
    on the Horse.

WHERE TO, O UNKNOWN SOUL,
O UNKNOWN UNIVERSE?

It, he, she, they, covered with a bright gold cloth,
it, the unknown dead body, was carried with light gold
as they ran soon after dawn, running, carrying
it, he, she, they, on a litter, it was as if there was already
a fire, running fast to the cremation ground and Ganga;

the unknown body was as light as the breath of
a living person.

BENARES

A dime a dozen—
more like a rupee
a thousand—any
way many most
millions by the Ganges,
young boys, thin, dark,
large eyes, smiling, waiting
to make a sell, offer for
a rupee or two all those
scented prayer necklaces,
the huge Sun is rising at
this very moment as
tourists in a daze buy
a dozen, as thousands
from all over India
or the Hindu world respond
actively respond with some
sort of yoga some sort of
hope to the wide river
and the expansive light.

BHUMISPARSHAMUDRA

I touch the ground
meaning I've been here before,
every plant has preached my
enlightenment.

BIRTHDAY POEM

Strike
OM
upon
the   Joy!
gong
you
beast
of

ON STAGE

"Do you
remember your speech?"
said the sea and the moon
the sand and the dragon the
tiger and the festival, death, sleep,
and cousins to the Reader-and-Writer.

"WHEN THE TIME CAME FOR THE GUARDIAN
ANGELS OF THE WORLD TO PROCLAIM
'THE BUDDHA UPROAR', WE ARE TOLD THAT
THE 'GODS OF ALL TEN THOUSAND WORLDS
CAME TOGETHER IN ONE PLACE', AND HAVING
ASCERTAINED WHO WAS TO BE THE BUDDHA,
PUBLICLY ACCLAIMED HIM AS SUCH."
—E. TOMLIN: *THE ORIENTAL PHILOSOPHERS*.

Like shafts of light about a flower
or the uprising of white birds from a rock in a
        northern sea
or the sudden dance of mermaids pronouncing names
        of our friends
or the outspoken assembly of the most lyric and
        mystic visitants
        to the United Nations

the guardian angels rushed upon You and baffled you
　　　　for Ever, but regaining
brighter Consciousness and instances and initiation of
　　　　syllables, AUM, Home, Home Run,
　　　　　　Raid, Save the raft of a very slight smattering of
　　　　　　gods of more than ten thousand worlds,
springing up with light on your hands
　　　　and all over our bodies
　　　　　　as We See Each Other
we joined the Buddha Uproar.

A Japanese Journal (1958-1965)

Sitting on a bench
on a sunny day in the breeze
with a series of beautiful Japanese women
I feel as if I am on a clothes line
with colored angels.

*

When
you find
the quintessence of poetry
your life becomes light,
your coat
doesn't weigh anything.

FISH OR SIR TO THE WATERY EXCITEMENT

I
always
feel
as   that's
if   what
I'm   I
in   call
                       intuition.

"THE FACT IS THE SWEETEST DREAM THAT LABOR KNOWS": ROBERT FROST

It's
true
and
I
yawned.
In
the
sun
at
Kokubunji
Station
reading
Robert
Frost.

A
Japanese
taxi
driver
stretching
himself
in
the
sun
for
some
international
reason
also
yawned.

Good
yawns
make
good
neighbors;
we
awoke
and
slept;
the
dream
also
is
the
sweetest

fact
that
labor
knows.
Not
only
this
but
bliss.

THE SWEETNESS OF DESTINY

Three women squatting cutting cabbages;
three fates preparing vegetable soup.

*

I thank you stone
that I sit on for upholding me.
I thank you air around me
for being inconspicuous, friendly, and present.
I thank you hand and pen for writing.
Things save us as we behold them.

DRIFTERS OR
OPULENT AND LIGHT LORDS IN WHITE WITH
NOT MUCH TO WORRY ABOUT OR DO

Several lords
huddled together
like several clouds
on a mountain
met to talk about
what they forgot
to talk about; then
someone yawned;
they remembered
to yawn; then
someone said
let us visit
the cherry trees;
they remembered
to follow;   some
looked at each
other looking
at cherry blossoms;
some fell asleep;
some drifted
away
like clouds.

A BOAT WITH A BLUE CANOPY IN A BUSY
STREAM WHERE MANY FISHING BOATS BY A
WATERFALL AND GREEN MOUNTAINS ARE
CARRYING THE HEROES TOWARD THE CATCH

Some sort of
lord meaning
some one who
can afford
somehow to sit
now in his dim
green kimono
is riding in
a long thin boat

with a blue
patch of heaven
over him as
it is getting
very dark
and a large
dim paper
lantern is
near him
as he watches
many lords
meaning now
fishermen in many
wooden boats
catching fish
via cormorants
and long lines of poetry.

*

The shadows
of the pine
tree on my desk
on my hand
on my happiness
are sending me messages
of yesterday's great rain
of my happiness last night.
The fish around Japan
are singing.

KYOTO IN THE SPRING

Umbrellas like flowers carried by girls,
rain like flowers carried by gods.

To
what
do
we
pay
homage
as
we
go
toward
our
spiritual
home ?
To
what
do
we
bow
as
we
grow

smaller
and
smaller
until
we
grow
bright
enough
to
enter
the
universe ?

WHEN SOMETIMES AWKWARDNESS
IS ALMOST FITTING

My
long
woolen
under
wear
follow
me
around
a
little
loosely
like
some
inexact
but
pleasing
thought.

PRAYER OR MONEY BOX

A Buddhist money box with kanji
like animated cartoons
animated the coins
until they or you become moons.
Walking by the moon
you carried a wooden prayer box
with your mother and father
sitting and singing in it like children.

BUDDHA INSPECTS BUDDHA

An ant
on the eyelid
of the god inspected
the insight of the stone.

SOMEWHERE A KIMONO IN THE MAKING

Strips of color
hanging out to dry
banners that will become dresses
later dresses that will become flying flowers.

*

He
could
not
cross
the
bridge

until
he
wrote
a
poem,
the
poem
being
the
bridge.

*

A
bee
settles
on
a
petal
of
a
cherry
blossom
in
the
pool
and
becomes
a
buddhist
ferryman.

*

Man in the dark
peeing against a wall in the rain
holding an umbrella over him
pleased with everything wet.

How   How
many   many
ants   Suns
are   are
crawling   in
in   a
the   syllable?
dark?

A WIDE DIM SCENE OF FARMERS SOME WITH WIDE HATS IN SUMMER EARLY IN THE MORNING IN THE VERY DIM RICE FIELDS BEGINNING THEIR WORK

dim in the
dim as when
we are satisfied
and waking up
on a summer
dim morning
dim in the dim
houses covered
with straw
sleepy dreamer
with a wide
hat of summer
dim in the
dim of these
dim houses
I see families
like sleep walkers
waking up and
eating and some
are walking
walking
towards the
dim stream
nearer you
to sit and
be sleepy and
happy on
a rock.

Every now and then
sitting on my
zabuton under a
light mountain of
blankets my foot
like a village at the
bottom of a mountain
begins to fall asleep
and I have to get up
and dance and shake
the church bells
in order to wake
the inhabitants.

*

Mountain
of Chinese noodles,
heaven for a poor man.

OFTEN WHEN THERE IS A STORM THE PETALS
OF FLOWERS THAT FLY THROUGH THE AIR
STICK TO THE WET STRAW RAINCOATS OF
TRAVELLING FARMERS

Farmers on a raft
in a flowery storm
see how you have
been wet to gather heaven.

ON THE ROAD OF SUCCESS

These
books of revelations

revealed riots in the weeds,
riots in words. The prophets
held up the syllables the way
mothers hold up babies, the way
mystic acrobats hold up the galaxies,
the way Lao-tzu and Lieh-tzu reveal the Way.
Along the road some beggars sat, slept and sang.

THE READER IS ENTITLED TO A TITLE

Several thoughts
revised
themselves
like gods
walking hand in hand
down the road
just laughing.

ON A CROWDED TRAIN ONE HOT DAY

An
old
man
from
the
sea
with
a
green
face
enters
the
subway
train
with
a
paper
bag

and
before
you
know
it
every
body
emerges
from
the
train
with
a
wet

smelling   fish.
of
fish

                    *

            The dangers
            like typhoons
            that stand at the Door of Love
            must be given flowers
            and called by the
            names of the gods.

ANCESTRAL PORTRAITS

                the
                mark
                of
                leaves
                in
                the
                flying
                air

Did
you
ever
let
a   it
poem   would
go   return
through   in
the   another
air   season
like   in
a   another
swift   life ?
beautiful
bird
not
asking
it
to
tell
a
word
knowing

VARIOUS STRAY READERS IN THE PATCHED UP COLORED COSTUMES OF LOVE JOIN A PROCESSION

A
gay
haphazard
procession
of songs   joy
and patches   proceeded
culminating   to
in   include
an   you.
open
paper
umbrella
with
flowers
and
birds
on
it
that
turns
with
the
speed
of

FRIENDSHIP

Sleep sat next to me
like a man on the subway.
Sleep said, Write a poem.
I said, you are a poem.
Sleep was my friend.
Always between places
we are closing our eyes
and growing. We are
always going towards
each other or poetry.

Sleep said, Have I written you?
You said, I am sleepy.

*

I cannot help but think
that we Lombards are related to the ancient Chinese.
I see it in the face of old peasants
and in their love of rice
and a certain sadness, sarcasm, humor.
The mistiness of the river Po
reminds me of the clarity and nearness of Li Po.

MAKING A COMIC BANQUET OF A WILD ONE

Dear wild fierce shark
the clever Chinese have put your fins into their soup
to finish you most exquisitely.

A STAR PERFORMER IN A JAPANESE FESTIVAL

Tight
rope
walker
with
the
umbrella
and
the
kimono
doing
the
strip
tease
and
going
through
hoops,
very
plump
and
transcendent
and
beautiful
Japanese

woman
now
in
a
sparkling
brassiere
with
ballet
tights
standing
on
one
leg
by
the
shrine

and
the
moon
and
a
thousand
admirers
like
the
dark

sea
watch
your
galaxy.

THE PINTA, THE NINA, AND THE SANTA MARIA;
AND MANY OTHER CARGOES OF LIGHT

America
I
carry
you
around   a
with   poem
me   growing
the   expanding
way   like
Buddha   a
carried   galaxy   the
a   the   way
grain   way   eloquence
of   a   carries
sand   firefly   hope,
the   carries   faith,
way   a   and
Columbus   galaxy   the
carried   the   4th
a   way   of
compass   Faulkner   July.
the   carries
way   eloquence
Whitman
carried

YOSHIWARA

under
one
kimono
is another
kimono is another
kimono and so on
so that colors representing
many butterflies in ecstasies
are found as one approaches
the gay quarters.

HOW MEMORABLE AND MUSICAL IS
THE SLOW PROCEDURE OF THE MOON

If
the
moon
could
walk
and
it
could
as   now
a   I
Noh   see
actor   it
upon   dimly
the   haunting
snow   me
of   with
my   beauty
sleep   in
it   the
would   morning
make   of
marks   my
perhaps memory.
like
the
shadows
of
pine trees

If one is
ever poor
go and see
the grass
just a few
delicate thin
young dim
green blades
of grass in
the breeze and
see as you
worship
these sages
the small
stars
of flowers
go a little
to the right
and see
the heavens
of small
blue flowers
and below
small white
flowers if
you are ever
king bring
this joy.

*

Sitting under a temple gate
thinking of a fish in the sea
thinking of a large crooked tree
thinking of the temple as an old wooden boat
we begin to float
anchored to the Sky.

A
Chinese
sage
like
a
Chinese
Theater
before   that
a   like
performance   Fire
like   or
infinite   the
bowls   Typewriter
of   said
rice   proceed.
was
surrounded
closely
by
a
very
amorous
Tiger

*

If one is not somewhat satisfied with silence
How will one enjoy a song ?
If someone is not somewhat satisfied with space
How will one enjoy a rose expanding ?

The Doorless Door (1958-1969)

Wide mountain going gently down to the lovely sea;
monk snoring.

GREY TILED ROOF IN A FLOOD OF RAIN

Fish on the roof
dreaming of the sea;
sea in the raindrop
dreaming of the fish.

HOTEI STOPS AND WONDERS

Philosophy flees;
fleas philosophize.

*

Chrysanthemums
several lions asleep in the dew.

GETA

Each person carries his own wooden
temple with him—
or a bridge on which he stands
under which the waters of time pass.

Various
whiskered
Chinese
sages
in
the
bushes
like
secrets
laughing
discuss
the
proper
temperature
of
sake.

ONDA

The
potter
at
his
wheel
repeats
Creation
like
a
tree
with
leaves.

*

a
beautiful
vase
is

round
so
we
can
wander
around
it
forever

MATSUKAZE: TWO FISHERGIRLS RECALL THEIR LOVE WITH THE MISSING POET AND HIS POEMS

Two
moons
remembering
slightly
meandering
on
the
Noh
stage
stage
a
comeback
therefore
the
dead
Poet
is
Revived.

His
poems
are
like
the
pebbles
on
the
shore
now
where
they
dance.

FROM THE NOH PLAY BY KANNAMI KIYOTSUGU
SOTOBA KOMACHI: "THE BRIGHTEST MIRROR IS
NOT ON THE WALL."

FROM YEATS: "FROM MIRROR AFTER
MIRROR NO VANITY'S DISPLAYED;
I'M LOOKING FOR THE FACE I HAD
BEFORE THE WORLD WAS MADE."

The
only
mirror   as
I   lightly
ever   as
knew   the   multiplied
was   golden   into
me   sun   the
or   bears   dance
you   poems.   of
and   The   God.
this   reflection
is   of
every   a
where   fish
to
bear

FROM THE NOH PLAY *ATSUMORI* BY SEAMI
MOTOKIYO: "LIFE IS A LYING DREAM, HE ONLY
WAKES WHO CASTS THE WORLD ASIDE."

I
did
this
but
soon
after   until
what   all   before
I   the   the
cast   galaxies   illusion   Effortlessly
there   and   of   the soul
became   gods   sleeping   resounds.
a   are   or
child   where   waking
poet   they   stirred
talking   were   effort.
all
night
long

The
joy
of
seeing
a
person
write
               the

a   world
child   begin
make
a
mark

the
joy
of
seeing

Being
so
being
being
so
present
being
so
beyond
if   question
you   and
ask   answer.
Ancient
China
about
its
happiness
being
so
near
being
so
dear
answered
being
so
being
you
are
the

A
Bodhisattva
sitting
for
a
painter
or
a
seed
sitting
for
the
Rain
or
a
circle
waiting
for
a
Musician
began
to
rise
carrying

Audience
and
Universe.

A VERY BRIGHT DAY AND ALL THE FUTON
ARE OUT TO RECEIVE AND PERCEIVE

Futon
out
the
window witnessing
like always
marvellous the
colored odd
heavy procession
flags between
in death
the and
sun life
absorbing walking
the and
dark sleeping.
dreams The
of colors
the of
Bright an
Head unknown
of eternal
the Ceremony.
Dreamer
the
Sun

THE VAGUE STEAM SEEMS TO COME FROM THE DRAGON IN A RESTAURANT ALL BOLD WITH RED AND BLACK AND GOLD SIGNS

A
large
Chinese
bowl
of flying
steaming designs
soup under
with the
a nose
long of
wild a
red small
dragon child.
some
sumptuous
birds
of
green
and
yellow
some

A MILLION PHOTOGRAPHIC FAMILIES BY BLOSSOMING BUDDHAS AND CHERRY TREES AT A CERTAIN COOL HEIGHT

A
funny
father
pictures
his
family
his
wife
in
green
and
purple
his
daughter
in
pink
and
orange
his
son
in
a
student
outfit
in
black

by
a
large
brown
wooden
temple
as
Buddha
in
the
dark
pictures
him.

A HERMIT IN AN OPEN HUT IN THE MOUNTAINS READS: "NOT KNOWING WHEN THE DAWN WILL COME, I OPEN EVERY DOOR" BY EMILY DICKINSON

Have
you
mentioned   I
the   see
mountain   them
to   entering
the   like
mountain   friends
the   at
mouse   the
to   doorless
the   door.
mouse
the
door
to
the
door?

*

Birds
were
singing
a
million   Suns
years   were
before   waiting
men   too   Poems
came   for   were
to   fathers   waiting
the   to   for
earth   bring   Readers.
to   them
hear   forth.
them.

AMIDST THE MILLIONS OF CROWDS ANYWHERE ON THIS SMALL PROLIFIC ISLAND, OR

THE HEROISM OF WHEN BEING ALONE MEANS BEING WITH EVERYONE-IN-CREATION

Being
alone   was
like   not
a   lonely
flower   but
unto   only   every where.
itself   another
in   sign
a   of
crowd   Buddha's
of   flowering
creation

THE TAOIST WAY TO CONFIDENCE

If
you   hide
confide   you   reveal
in   the   you
the   way   the
universe   a   way
it   bride   a
will   hides   need
confide   a   reveals
in   seed   the
you   it   universe.
it   will
will

THE STORY OF SUMI

a
pine
tree
burnt
became
ashes
and
from
these
ashes
awoke
a
sage
called
sumi

who
sold
his
brushes
in
China
and
Japan.

T'ang
sang
Kanji
became
king.

A
man
who
doesn't   pushing
eat   his
much   way
but   through
heavenly   the   space
rice   tangled   wandering
is   dim   this
standing   thick   way
in   busy   towards
a   weeds   heaven.
long   is
thin   in
boat   this
in dim   scene
blue   of
with   mostly
a   dim
long   and
pole   white
and
strong

AN OLD CHINESE ZEN TRAVELLER OFTEN DEPICTED IN SUMI-E CARRYING A LARGE DIM WHITE BAG LIKE A LIGHT CLOUD

Hotei
has
his
own
hotel
with
him
also
his
own
mountain
also
his
own
sleep
also
his
own
Zen
also
his
own
weather

and
whether
you
like
it
or
not
also
our
own
galaxy.
Clouds
may
imitate
him.
Birds
may
migrate
to
him.

Zen
may
repose
in
him.
But
nevertheless
no
concept
or
poem
is
his
hotel.
Hotei
laughs
at

him-
self-
and-
you.

IHARA SAIKAKU: *THE ALMANAC-MAKER'S BEAUTIFUL WIFE*: "HER MOON SHAPED EYEBROWS RIVALLED IN BEAUTY THE CRESCENT BORNE ALOFT IN THE GION FESTIVAL PARADE; HER FIGURE SUGGESTED THE CHERRY BUDS, NOT YET BLOSSOMS, OF KIYOMIZU; HER LOVELY LIPS LOOKED LIKE THE TOPMOST LEAVES OF TAKAO IN FULL AUTUMNAL GLORY."

Fortunately
her
calendars
and
stellar
qualities
were
known
in
the
dark
by
many
festivals,
lanterns,
lovers
and
fireflies.

Her
husband
working
on
his
designs
did
not
know
the
common
symbolism
of
his
stirring
thoughts.

And
as
he
indicated
lucky
days
having
had
magnificent
nights
the
calendar
all
bright

and
festive
and
lucky
indicated
her
beauty
experienced
throughout
the
year.

SLEEPY STANDING IN THE SUNNY
WINDY KOKUBUNJI STATION

After
a
night
of
rain
like
an
old
rubber
boot
I
tried
to
dry
in
the
sun
like
a
lover

drenched
and
battered
with
music
like
a
sheep
just
dropped
out
of
sleep
musing
on
the
madness
of

beauty.
I
could
not
nor
would
not
reason
about
the
season
but
the
sun
asked
only

that
it
be
the
sun.
All
out
we
gathered
the
syllables.
A
dozen
people

or
more
in
the
gay
mad
wind
walking
on
high
geta

IS THE WORD HERE OR HEAVEN?

Neither
sadness
nor
joy   or
but   the
emptiness   word
then   reappears
the   on
world   a
will   page
reappear   after
the   the
way   poet's
a   visit
child   to
appears   Here.
in
the
womb

The China Travel Journal (1984)

CROWDED SHANGHAI MARKET INCLUDING
AND SURROUNDED BY MANY VEGETABLES
AND TRUCKS AND BICYCLES

Slop from the sea, slime, slithering, a million tiny eels,
  elves upon
the butchers' tables, fantasies about to be cut, slippery, and
  devoured,
hour after hour and century after century, the centaurs or
  seamen
squat, square off, squander, prepare a thousand Chinese suppers,
  slight drizzle,
mother eels fester, festoon, squid, crabs, fish not yet catalogued
  by scientists
or metaphors, seas sliding, Proteus drowsy, dolphins diving,
  more fish arriving,
the tides tremble, the crescendos of rivers enter the sea,
  the nets are plentiful,
the Shanghai fish market stinks to high heaven, Marxist
  or not,
the profit motive of fish proceeds, in the wet active time many seek,
  search, nibble,
to be hooked, cooked, bowls of undecipherable Chinese hieroglyphics
  from the deep seas,
handy, the marketeers squash in their wet hands the prolific
  forefathers;
catching, selling, and eating we enter the ancient routine
  of the new day.

SCATTERING DYNASTIES ALONG THE WAY

What about "saving" the world today ? can you do it by
  reading a poem from
  the Tang period ?
why not ? so then start. Or start by confronting the
  mosquito or a wish for a
  summary that is about
  to annoy you.
Is it all there to annoy you or start you—Moses, those
  phrases in poems, those glances from the
  different tribes ?

Recently I was saving the world
by going three times to see the great paintings
by the eight eccentrics of Yangjhou.
It could take time to save it, if you're going to do it in
haiku or epics or travel journals;
you might suddenly realize
by planetary motion that you are far flung, that you
are the dancer whose very dreams
and gestures are giving it a
wish or a push.

CONCERNING THE ANCIENT SILK ROUTE

For a long time keeping the silk worm a secret and
not even knowing
the secret itself of the silk worm or the self, the conniving
and imaginative and playful
Chinese merchants made up stories to send off to foreigners
in different directions,
some saying silk grew on trees, some saying it resulted
from coupling waves and
tall grass at certain moments during moonlit nights,
other stories have been forgotten;
nevertheless the silk worms in their multiplying mulberry
leaves munched, proceeded,
millions of Chinese had lunch and laughter, Marco Polo
returned to fabulous Italy
with more fables.

5 PM AND MORE THAN 5 MILLION

A cold wind, and more than a million bicycle wheels,
Shanxi Lu,
mandala and greyness and February wind moving,
dampness,
and a million people on bicycles going home from
work, a certain
destined gliding, centuries wheeling, it seems effortless,

a baby now and then,
often, bundled up in many colors and with a bright woolen hat,
    wide like little emperors
carried noodles cooking, thousands with bowls in their
    Chinese hands,
Marco Polo, you were right; posters of tooth paste and
    movies, transistors, a new
consumer society beginning years after a necessary great
    Revolution; the seasons are
revolving, the trees line the immensely immensely crowded
    wide avenues; noodles
being eaten in the customary peasant-and-imperial manner;
    Spring is coming.

AT THIS KNOWLEDGE AND IN
THIS KNOWLEDGE CONSUMMATION

If you are quiet enough deep and active in meditation
    in sympathetic attention
you will discover there is a sound to everything and in the
    sound you might be
prophetic enough to discover the object and your state of
    being related to it; the Ming poet
Chang Yu just told me "smelling and hearing are really the same thing"
    and "the fragrance sends
forth jewel-like songs." Consequently the microcosm of our
    sensuous knowledge
confirms and informs us very richly. In such vitality even universes
    are hinted at.

I JUST READ A POEM BY YANG CHI ABOUT
BEING IN HIS STUDIO "LISTENING TO THE SNOW"

The Chinese listening to tones—
        of their subtle vowels and voices,
        varied and chirping and colloquial in the streets,
Yang Chi from the Ming Dynasty and thousands of other poets from other
        times and places, he from Suchou,

listening to the rain, listening to
silence, to the night, to the
falling of leaves, to the
motions and notions of water, streams, dreams, to the arrival of
a friend, a perhaps
expected reader.

AWAKENING WE SEE THE AIR, WE SEE THE LIGHT

Sakyamuni peacefully profoundly smiling
has achieved miles of bliss in our sleep.

*

The northern Wei Buddha was smirking
very much, it was his way.

YANG-CHU'S REPUBLIC

The prize is the life of this mosquito
and his follower Yang-chu, and
my following you; left alone we
bargain with the universe, we wonder
that this procreation has festivals;
we join in; this nature is my republic.

DOING ONESELF A HEAVY WRONG
INSTEAD OF A LIGHT SONG

The worried ambitious man was weighing results,
accumulating burdens that way, becoming ponderous,
this was not the way of Chuang-tzu *wu wei*

*

I was giving all I had at the moment
but since you had more I was giving
all I had at the next moment and
since the moment was part of your
        immortality
we couldn't speak about accomplishment,
        end or beginning

*

It is just natural to want to be original
and to actually be original, for it is that
which is the source of change, of death, of life,
of festival, of families, of momentary discoveries.
The Middle Kingdom is always being centralized.
America and the reader are always being discovered.

REVIVAL OF POWER

Ancient musical instruments,
wake up, tomorrow's Chinese composer,
play again way back way ahead in the
        cosmic Moment

the Sounds to stir the thoughts of all the sleeping
gods past, present, future.

DEER BIRD, DEAR BIRD / MIDDLE KINGDOM, CENTRAL QUEENDOM

Stork or phoenix,
fire or elongated erection, keep up
the crooning, keep up
    the civilization,
herald the dawn right in the
    center of Dawn.

INSTRUMENTS THAT MUST HAVE BEEN ORIGINS OF GAGAKU AND KOTO INSTRUMENTS

Girl guardian huddled in the cold grave museum,
introspective way back to what is the
origin of the Middle Kingdom,
everybody's central Art.

I HAVE MY FISH WISHES TOO

Fish,
you have your fish wishes,
you swerve according to the Tao.
Hungry, slippery, accomplished.

RESPONDING TO SCULPTURE IN
THE SHANGHAI MUSEUM

Pressing one's feet on the lotus,
pressing one's feet on the dream,
the lotus is not crushed, the Bodhisattva
helps himself and us and it Blossom.

MOMENTOUS AND ETERNAL

Standing at attention, attending to the rules
        from within,
the buddhas are ruled by the flower of the hour.

EVENTS IN THE PEACEFUL SKY

Tu Fu: "Our poems will be handed
Down along with great dead poets."
I know we are ambitious, that is trivial.
I admire seeds being carried by the wind,
the future unknown sons who climb tree tops
        and whistle.

*

Keeping a delicate balance in traffic difficulties:
millions of people on bicycles well-centered.

The fingers do not rebel in being fingers,
the toes do not rebel in being toes,
the right ear and the left ear accept their places,
the nose is well placed in the Middle Kingdom;
cooperation at a constructive game
one inspires, we build a house.

THEY STAND FOR GOOD NOURISHMENT, THEY STAND FOR ENDURING ART

Huge bronzes, more sturdy than squat warriors,
bold squat strong bronzes, stronger than soldiers,
outlasting weather and centuries; earth centered
heavy really present ancient bronzes, more than modern;
sources of nourishment; domestic, tribal, tremendous;
    artful and practical.

CHUNG, HEAVY, NOTHING FLIMSY HERE . . . WUHAN BELLS

Bronze bells, tones, tons of tones,
vibrations from the center of mountains,
vibrations from between mountains,
vibrations sturdy as dreams of priests.
Hear what the cycles, centuries and gods have to say.
Chimes to rime with endurance. Middle Kingdom,
    Central Musicians.

WUHAN RECALLED

Of course it is an amusement park,
the dragon's back, the dragon is back,
the dragon is all changing colors, became
when the fancy and flames spread many
dragons of many colors suddenly swaying,

dancing like all Chinese New Years, you
were in on it, inside the moving colors,
your desire and newness renewed the festival
after many years, the dancer splurged again,
the cymbals banged, the drums were vigorous,
the four dragons from each corner of the world
and the Imagination rampaged strongly to pursue the
sun.

*

Finding myself in all the living creatures
I join the immortals.

*

When I was born I saw ten thousand bicycles, that's
        putting it mildly,
when my grandmother held me I saw ten million
        bicycles, that's more
accurate, astrologers can take account of cycling
        destinies, astronomers
can take account of moving galaxies; I reach out for my
        relatives who take me for a ride.

ABOVE THE FAR EXTENDED BRANCH IS A POEM, BELOW THIS CELEBRATION IS A POEM

A long a very long thin branch delicate very long and
        miraculously strong
with some first plum blossoms extends and extends
        itself east and west,
you are the best at first seeing and flowering.

CHINESE BICYCLES WITH SPIRITUAL
LEADERS BY THE MILLIONS

I'm sure of that—
those wheels are still turning—the millions that I haven't
     seen
and the millions that I have seen, that passed me by while
     I was walking,
that I passed by when riding in a crowded bus;
     sometimes the bicycles
were carrying furniture, sometimes ducks, often seated
     in front was a tiny calm
child like a satisfied buddha; now that's what I wonder
     about and want to learn from—
the source of that blissful riding satisfaction; a familiar
     scene which sets me wheeling.

LEARN FROM THE BEST PERFORMERS

When dinosaurs had their youthful age millions of
     years ago, when
the native sun was still hot in their feet and cosmic
     commotion, when
they stomped so that they were the origin of
     world rhythm, when
their tongues still were like flames from the
     father sun, and when
these leviathans of the Chinese vast lands and
     excited mountains were
active like volcanoes, when their footwork and
     bending instructed the
first Chinese musical scores, really loud and
     festive, were they not
then what now we call dragons ? don't drag on
     a pedantic answer but
put on a costume or more than three thousand poems
     and Perform.

TAI-YANG MEANS SUN AND YUAN
CHEN'S POETRY MEANS PLEASURE

On my green deck behind my Abbott Street house
       I sit Oriental fashion
by 3 rows of many pots, one to my left side, one to
       the back, one to the front,
each pot with many sturdy small marigolds. T'ai-yang,
       a relative of theirs and mine,
       is making my back and
       the green deck warm.

WHILE READING "TO THE WATERS
OF CHIA-LING" BY YUAN CHEN

The clear stream from nearby has come from far away, its
       waters, their murmurings,
and my memories, and my stream of consciousness, are like
       you in that way;
we are fluent in our relationships and as clear as possible.

THE NARCISSUS IN CHINESE PAINTING
OFFERS THE PROMISE OF SPRING

He did not love himself as separate from his
       love of painting
or as separate from his love of you or of his
       love to have you love his
paintings; dim and delicate and fine and sturdy and everywhere ,
       sturdy as grass or an
unseen god or the juice in the stem; Chao Meng-Chien
       of the Southern Sung Dynasty,
accomplished scholar and calligrapher, specialized in
       painting narcissi.

CHINESE GUIDE BOOK: "THE LARGEST BUDDHA HAS AN EAR TALLER THAN THE HEIGHT OF AN AVERAGE MAN."

To hide in his ear
> and then come out
> to tell the object about the soul;
to take our measure
> by his long ear which
> signifies longevity;
here at Longmen to hear the scriptures
> by seeing these thousands
> of buddhist images;
listening at Longmen to brides, wind, leaves of grass,
> the river, the people, the
> bright air above us;
to take our measure here by the length of his
> immortality.

SOMEWHAT THOUGHTS AMIDST RUSTLING AUTUMN LEAVES

I don't regret that I can't be a scholar of the
> poets of the T'ang, Sung,
Yuan, Ming, Ch'ing, and other Dynasties, there are
> so many ! and
they wrote so many thousands of poems, but as a
> somewhat exiled loafer
I can leaf and live through their pages, now and
> then enjoy reading
some of their poems; doing that and now and then hearing
> the song of a bird or the sound
of a stream or enjoying the colors of the seasons—*sometimes*
> that's exactly enough for me.

When the long winged bird brings its wings
      together
and perches high in the tree seeing the world
      it is somewhat
like closing a book of poems after you have
      read them all.

TRANSFORMING CROWDS OF BODHISATTVAS PATIENTLY AWAITING

I always
forget his name
but he was a Chinese monk
who came back with the sutras,
a backpack of scrolls to enlighten the world,
      came back
from a long trek to India, to somewhat follow
      the pathless
path of his thought would be a journey to lift
      the soles of the
best travellers. To balance the budget, the budding
      buddhism, there was
a little bell distended over his bald head projecting
      from his backpack,
projecting high over his nose, so that the scrolls would
      be properly maintained
as he walked hundreds of miles on deserts and mountains;
      a little tinkling now and
then with higher education reminds us that it's often time
      to say our prayers and praises
      for the transforming clouds.

To wake up
      early on a
      Spring morning when the light is
      very delicate and somewhat warm and yet
      cool enough and dip into a book of non-assertive
      poetry, this dawn for instance by Mo Shih-lung,
reminds me of a bird coming out of the forest and dipping itself
      in a fountain and shaking its wet wings as
      it flies in the brightness.

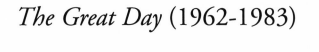

The Great Day (1962-1983)

ACT

From way up there
you jumped through
a loop of fire or a hoop of sunlight
or the sound of invisibility (and invincibility ?)
into a small pool
and then through that as through music through to another pool
and on into another pool and so on, no one can call
you a fool for doing that with your particular
lyrical upsurge, it was necessary,
like the appearance of the moon,
like the singing of the sun,
it was also tell anyone
like looking at a
flower

JANUARY 2

I offer you my presence, world,
it is a mutual admiration society, including stars and species,
          including grains of wood and Shakespeare,
as you offer me your presence, world,
we take It on the go; we go together whether we seem to or not
          the way true husband and wife do
          the way Adam and Eve and your great grandchildren do,
chanting these offerings
          to the bees
          and forefathers
          and previous poets
          and the clouds and rivers and roads
we see that the world has many people bowing and leaping
          being born and sleeping;
from the very center of your sleep's Sleep and your awakening's
          Awakening
give forth the secrets of courtesy to the approaching
          and disappearing
friends, gods and relatives.

SOME SORT OF "*LIEDER*"

Where is the muse hiding ? you don't exactly
        feel urged to write a poem
and yet you do, you're not quite awake; what
        about you, reader ?
the day outside is tremendously cold and vastly grey,
        and it looks as if
it might snow; are you waking up and hoping for
        music, the kind
that performs every action sacramentally and is non-
        possessive and shelters
the muse ? I thought I heard ancient friends
        thinking of her at the same time that
        I was thinking of them.

THE GIFT OUTRIGHT

They aren't demanding
though they excite my glorious glance,
they aren't expecting you to act in a
        certain way towards them
though they are recurring and certainly
        ample and generous,
the colors of the autumn leaves.

THE BLOSSOMING OF ORIGINAL IDENTITY

And so the scent of the rose is sent to us
        when necessary,
we take a whiff and wonder while closing our eyes
        of the infinite
which makes the blossoming a complete universe.
        Not a statement given
such as a love note but love itself in which
        the lovers find
each other floating; Tiepolo's angels trumpet our

heroism. Easy
as watching the rose expand or noticing the clouds
in their adventures.

"WHAN THAT APRILLE . . . "

Two bicycles
like the birth of flowers
whirl on the spring day, what suns in the Word
make the wheels spin ? lovers with skies for customs
        take a dip into
surprise, coolness;   the great grass by the side
        of the riders
is preparing its lectures;   the great trees by the side
        of the riders
are preparing their canopies;   those popes the birds
        are outdoing already
        theologians; when
the bicycles begin to go, zig zag a bit, hit the
        air like hail,
and the spokes are buzzing but somewhat unseen like
        future poems,
when they dart in the heaven of now
        Hallelujahs
        applaud.

THE GRACIOUS HEROINE HELPS
THE DANCER BECOME FREE

        To choose
        one word or choose another word
        the astronaut makes his decision

        to choose
        one flower or another blossom
        the bee makes its papal decree

to choose
one game or to choose a higher
the lover's ascending degree

Romeo on the balcony,
the green winged Gabriel by the Rose;
I am beckoned by your Courtesy.

JULY IN MAINE

Summer and
people are walking without any coats,
it's more like making love naked; the air caresses,
        the body is pleased by its own feelings,
        you are aware of its glow,
just as a plum knows it's a saint without being told—
        by the halo of light around it
        and because of its colors, that
        which symbolists call
        inner reflections,
the body of the person walking in light loose clothes
        knows the day loves it and
        that it loves the day
        and later it will love
        the night just as
        easily;
whenever love's rapport is so flowery and fruitful,
delicious and delicate and beautiful
we can call it summer.

I WANT TO KNOW WHO YOU ARE, NEW POET

I want to know who you are, new poet, so I read on and on.
I wonder who will I meet around the corner,
I wonder what conversation will be like
        the expansion of an angel's wings
        when we meet going from one
        Greek island to another,

I wonder who it will be, what strangeness, from which the words
        of Athena will ring pure and clear
in the foreign country, on the streets that I am
        forever walking
in search of the newness of the poem that is in
        any person.
You appear to me holding a laurel branch and I shake
        with laughter and we find
a wine shop by the sea and drink; and then our
        sleep will celebrate the
        gods; it is
very late, we need this surprise, this newness.

THE SUICIDE OF EVERY MAN

1.
In the Sun a man is hanging,
in the darkness a sun is dying.

2.
DEAN OF MEN

I do not know who is walking through the fire
I do not know who is walking on the snow in the fog
I do not see faces
I do not hear voices
but I see bodies lost in these days of many murders and suicides
and of wars, wars, and machinery, and weariness, staleness,
industry, people very busy and exhausted,
and newspapers
but I see someone walking down the corridor
and there are filing cabinets and coffins and burnt students
and filing cards and windows that look upon cars and snow
and I see someone slowly walking in a hospital
past doors and behind those doors the insane
and the sad and the speechless
I see someone knowing the myth of Sisyphus and trying
to move the stone and always finding a dead body under
the stone and next morning after breakfast moving
the same stone and finding another dead body
until all the dead bodies in the cremation ground

become the stars that are burning in his bones as he walks
as he sees all those dying
as he dies slowly as he goes to the basement to commit suicide
I see every man walking through the fire
I hear every man in the stone
in the dust

3.

Seated in the office
looking in a million mirrors
of one's many sicknesses, the cousins gone mad, the students .
        with their problems,
the vague of the lost in the lost of all generations,
seated seeing the grades of agony,
        the necessary degradations,
        the necessary rejections,
        the necessary abjections, cutting criticisms,
        the necessary fears of failure and all the little
        perversities that flesh is heir to, sitting
and watching in the fluorescent lit mirrors the graves of
        students flown back from the Vietnam war,
watching the lost and confused and weeping parents
        getting in and out of cars,
impersonal letters, advertisements, catalogues, reading the
        abstractions in the news,
concerning the murder of Jack Kennedy, of his brother, of
        Martin Luther King,
hearing the dead wailing and seeing all the lost students
        the Mirrors made the Eyes Bleed,
        made a Suicide for the World.

AMERICAN COMPLICATED WITH
INTEGRITY: HOMAGE TO MURIEL

It is difficult to see in this harsh light, in the glare of
        this machine place
with the ferocity of blandness, pollution, steel, trains and cars
        with tired people almost well adjusted
        to their lack of direction and

their routine; Kafka is in
his grave; Camus lets out another call as he falls; the river is
cold; the 385 dream songs are pieces of ice;
the Lewiston factories are making Marsden Hartley cumbersome and
outraged again; once more he celebrates
the splash of the uplifted Atlantic wave and the terror and songs of
Hart Crane; Homage to those shaken seers
on Main Street; the cars
ride by, the energy crisis, the identity crisis, the failure of
communication crisis; how can you forget
the concentration camps
and all that went with them ? but look at Muriel I say to my students,
look at Muriel Rukeyser,
collect her large volume of poems, she has protected, with those
activists we have overcome, the Song goes on;
her poems have collected our hope and power, to walk with
her and them makes us see bold incorrigible
indivisible Whitman ahead.

TWO ALSO RELATED TO FALSTAFF

MY AND PAOLO UCCELLO'S BATTLE SCENES AND
"QUELLA BENEDETTA PROSPETTIVA!"

How many of your selves are bleeding on the battlefield,
picturesquely, for centuries it seems,
for dreary days, for days of
deep depression ?
why so much brow-beating contention, bone-breaking self-doubt
and nightmares, the Fiend
strikes with invisible clubs turning my selves into illusions
a field of fog, making me
imagine I hate myself or that I have been drained of all
grand opera; but Verdi, green green, writes
another score, Falstaff bounds up,
Fullness Abounds so that it cannot
be caged, caught, or comprehended. Minions of Grace, gallants
of the gods, resume the battle,
Stage a come-back; comedy says "Give me life; which if I can
save, so; if not, honor comes unlooked for . . ."
and here's a Beginning . . .

That's the way I like a person,
impossible but brave, good,
incorrigible but present.

LETTER OF RECOMMENDATION

It turns out that the person that they (the magazines and Clichés
        and their academic followers) called a barbarian
was very courteous, civilized, refined, good looking, generous,
        skillful, gentle, a fast runner,
a fantastic dancer, a dreamer, one who could in his sleep remember
        the entire epic history of the race,
one who could in his waking moments touch her in such a way
        as to mention kingdoms,
one who was far sighted, so entranced, so endearing, such a
        gentleman, such a representative
of tactful admiration and an accomplished improvisor that he
        nodded to Montaigne's sentence
which goes something like this: "Thereby we may see
        how we should be on our guard against
        clinging to vulgar opinions . . ."
If anyone is shot by tacit consent or direct or indirect
        hatred or slightest prejudice you are a cannibal.

THE AGED AND THE DIAMOND

Ah, so there it is,
the earth and its Three Mysteries;
the old man, once Proteus, dolphin and sport, once millionaire
        of courtesy and though substantial
        light on his feet,
now one foot, one leg almost dead, he drags it as he walks slowly
        surrounded by the blaze of autumn days
seasons of splendor, orange, red, yellow, fire and history in every
        leaf; there he sits
strangely holding his sleepy kingdom, watching on TV a

baseball diamond
and the Dodgers and the Yankees
like the Achaeans and the Trojans
or like gods in battle
or Xanthus and Achilles:
one arm like a Church relic, he focuses his attention
on the young heroes
trying to make the home run
praising them as heavily lightly
he breathes—Heaven.

SEQUENCE: POEMS IN PRAISE OF MY FATHER

AFTER ANOTHER SLIGHT SPASM OR STROKE

What did he look like
as we rode smoothly by quietly in the Ambulance
from the Hospital to the Nursing Home called the Lamp
somewhat out in the country, anyway past trees and motels
on the Lisbon Road ? shades of Conquistadores, old sailings to
          this Mystery,
this not yet cultivated land, this now mostly polluted land.
     My Father
was not corrupted. When they lifted him, heavy, delicate, from the
          hospital bed and wrapped him in pink sheets
also making a pink cowl around his head and then putting
          heavy dark blankets on him he was mostly asleep
          though slightly at times he moved his eyelids
          and his Eyes which are Magnificent and Large and Great
          now looked small and blurred, when the two
          ambulance men lifted him from the bed
          I thought of Christ taken from the Cross.
He has a Strong and Big and Round Skull. Toothless. Mouth sunk in.
     At times it seemed no breathing, at times
     breathing slightly noisily like a sick whale.
I sat near him in the ambulance
as we floated almost noiselessly on the slightly winding
          road
past all the food places and motels and trees and gasoline stations;
          what
          Eternity
was I Attending? A Giotto stranger on the sidelines; a

Donatello Prophet wrapped in pink;
it seemed like a long quiet ride on the North Atlantic (though
        I made conversation with the Ambulance attendant
        about his profession).
Finding the right entrance to the Lamp they entered
        carrying my Father.

AFTER MANY PIETÀ SCENES

O fish

I can't control you out there in the sea

any more than I can my father in the

        Nursing Home

        who may be dying . . .

Comet, knock at a window ?

Clown, look at the clover ?

The skull is like the world;   and now those Eyes

        those Eyes

        those Eyes

those Eyes revealing the Great Soul   O as substantial

        as Falstaff   Sophocles

        peasants   peasants

a lilac bush is weeping

        those eyes can hardly open now

what can I do ?

what can I do ?

be literary about a fish in the sea ?

and give all my life

AFFECTIONATE BEYOND ALL MEASURE
BEYOND ALL REASON

Blowing the nose
trumpeting elephant
my Father not self-conscious
except when he is flirting

Ecological as all Eden

Accepting conventions gracefully, enacting courtesy naturally, not
    subservient to conventions, not rebellious at all,
as butler in Princeton he was a mysterious Prince,
    as active restaurant owner in New Jersey
    surrounded by trees and sometimes troubles
he was active and at times beggar, never abject or sordid, never
    twitchy nervous introspective,
by beggar I do not mean that he begged but that sensual as he was
    he knew about nothing,
most of his friends dead, for many years he played cards with them,
    often he took care of some when they were sick or dying,
    sometimes at one of the many funerals, Masonic or otherwise, he
attended
    he would say "here goes Nothing"

L'IVRESSE DE PROFONDEUR

Often these days
though I go about my routine and the days are bright
I do not feel as if I can wake

as if you and I are miles down in the sea
walking with heavy uniforms and searching some heavy treasure
        Some Trunk of the Universal Unconscious
        (let's tell Jung) (you didn't bother to ask me who he is)

we seem to understand each other way down there
        and our bodies like astronauts
        are buoyant beyond Boehme and champagne

133

I like the way you held a glass of champagne
          or of red wine up and
          drank to some friend
          and celebration

all the fish around us are like so many galaxies
          and they understand too

SWAYING IN POETIC RHYTHM

by the sound of the sea late at night
when I was small and you visited us after work
you pushed me on a swing
and I had been playing all day
by the breeze and the spray and the sun and the sea shells
and I was in the balmy atmosphere
and often going up feet towards the stars
way below the sound of your voice and friends
and you pushed me into that happiness
and I fell asleep and flew on to the sand
and somehow didn't get hurt
and you carried me home by the sea to bed

today by the sea in Maine
I thought of you and tonight in my high studio
in darkness I remember the sense of warmth and oneness
          we had with my mother and the sea spray
          and some friends and the evening

MY MASTERPIECE

take this hand   spusa

I touch you marrying you in New Jersey after we travelled over
          the seas that even Prospero couldn't describe

and see you

my dove

          my dove

          my great flying pure dove

better than Noah saw saw the bird   better than old
      and new testaments

in your gown of rice
in your gown of tears

in your gown of future children

in your gown of future children dreaming of angels

let me hide
let me find my more than America

           ****

           (*spusa* is the Lombard
           word for *sposa*—bride)

THE SPRAY OF THEIR SAYINGS WAS
ALWAYS TO BRING UPRISINGS

Returning with a bundle in her arms
      over all seas
      over all the skies
      over all the sighs
      over all the worries
      over all the songs of foam
      now and then surrounded by small clouds
                or large sea gulls
      now and then sung to by dolphins
      now and then a saint would leap out of the sea
      and quickly give the child a present
      infinite   indivisible   to be predicted
Returning with a child of fears and laughter
      of dreams and gods
      to the Maker of Feasts
      to the Welcomer of Friends
my Mother carrying a Mystery over the 7 seas
      said as the Boat Docked
      "Here he is, Battista,
      what a trip !"
O he had a whiff early in life of sea weed and mermaids' songs
      of legends from wet saints
      from Barnacle Bill the Mystic
      and from determined dolphins.

THE MANY WAYS OF PLAYING AND OF WATERING
A LAWN CAN BE LIKE FRESHMEN TEACHING RELIGIONS

With the long hose after watering the patches of lawn, the patches
        of poetry, the patches of forests,
the patches of fantasy and idyll around your restaurant, spraying
        at length at width carefree as a lark
        the countries of trees
their changing thoughts around your restaurant, squirting water
        happily widely lightly on the
great green house itself, as a growing boy with all sorts of secret
        games and stories and buried treasures
        and codes and swings,
I was "useful"—you laughed—you even paid me to do this wet
        and wandering and cool work; there were patches of
        "forget me nots" of lilies of the valley
        of large surprising irises
surrounding your restaurant and some small trees with very wide leaves;
        later on I would read and celebrate Whitman;
        now I was content
and generous and cavorting and your Eternal Assistant sprinkling the
        living land and its dreams and skies.

"I PREFER NOT TO DRIVE IN A
MECHANISM" THE COSMIC SPORT SAID

"we have to go to the dump and unload first"
I heard some workers say via some mechanical system

I was trying to write poems, recalling my Father
and they across the street in the cool morning light
were turning on and off some noise pollution, some mechanical system,

some like to send statistical static and messages from Texas
or from Kyoto or Hoboken or the Moon, it's their mechanical syndrome,
they have to "know how" and they make out that "progress" of all the
        information in Time Magazine and in the Soviet Banalities
        and that "progress" is all the junk East and West

my unpossessive Father with a sense of grace never ruined Eden

REUNION

"I hear you were having some pasta asciutta
and I decided to come back"; as we ate often
        during his life he reminded me when
        the glasses were almost empty
        to pour more red wine into them.

WHILE FUTURE ALTAR BOYS ARE
STARTLED BY THE AUTUMN WIND

There
at the back of my mind like a large actor capable of
        many disguises ready to go on stage
        is my Father;
in all kinds of moods, fearful, fretful, calm, humorous,
        in all kinds of weather
—now it was suddenly very dark and windy and there was a
        burst of rain—
I think of him—also like the Prompter; if I forget
        my lines he will
saunter along and slip me a liturgy; I will remember
        his patience his great patience
        those 17 years somewhat paralyzed
        like our century,
remember him after lunch after my mother rested
        from the intense lyricism of preparing
        lunch and eating it with connoisseur husband
how he quietly like some collection of altar boys
        back stage put away the dishes,
        put things in order, and then
        returned to his throne.

WHO NEEDS A REQUIEM?

        Large One
        Procession
        Bishop and all the Works

I never felt you left the Church any more than the Church could leave God

though you seemed to leave your parents at the age of 13
they sang in your thoughts like peasant-angels in the field

137

your mother worked at making her lace
           at making a place for the whole tribe near God
           and helped us See His Face

your gruff father farmer harvested plenty and holidays and
           Gave It To His Sons

fig trees and a few horses, a few hay stacks, dew and dawn,
           roosters roistering, and all
           the mysteries of birth-and-death

        you and I played priests comically
        as only those who love the priesthood can

Requiems, I don't have any thing against them; Fauré, Bach; Magnificat;
           Duccio, Cimabue; the wonders of Byzantium;

but you so largely at Peace   like the angels working in the dew
           of Your Father's Field
           did not really need them
           at times some of the lesser lights do

        DECEMBER   1970

        You never frightened me

        and you were never oppressive

        I do not find you looming   you did not plant guilt

           you never put moral meanings

           around our necks like Ideals or tomb stones

        You are never a weight

        I do not think your body can decay

        and your mind is not like a Library or School of Philosophy

           or an Engineering Building

        You were fully here

You were largely present

You do not hang around like a Puritan or Stoical Corpse

saying do this or finish that

You didn't even mind my preaching (this sort of stuff)

You could accept it

the way the holy universe accepts Christmas

You were not wilful and you made no slaves

BEYOND THE FIRST LIGHT AND
THE FIRST DARKNESS

I will dance in your restaurant for the rest of my life

and may I dance before you in Heaven

you will without will give thorough approval and

shake a little with laughter

whenever there is a new born flower   we will acknowledge it

and we will in parody

play at chants and processions   O my inventor

O my Invention

I see you proceeding where there are no graves

EXITS, SURPRISES, ENTRANCES

When we enter the great galaxy
          of the many bees and fish and sandpipers
          the vast distances   darkness

we perform our imitations; and others at the same time
        and before and after
are imitating us; it is a very vast darkness and we put
        on our shows, take a rabbit out of a hat,
        invent an alphabet,
        walk on a tight rope,
make higher mathematics, interpret metaphors, eat,
        sleep, eat, make love,
and all during this time a thought is imitating Krishna,
        Buddha is imitating a bee,
a child draws a picture of a sacred Fish, a housewife
        makes a wish,
religions are born like so many wandering fish; the galaxy
        like a Troupe of Actors
        performs for a few years
(accompanied by saints, angels, imitators, wonderers) in the wind
        . . . the traveling wind . . .

AFTER THE QUIET RAIN

Finding the true word which creates us is like finding the parents,
        the solitude is not literary though we can think of it
        as a long novel, novelty that keeps us
        going across the desert or across the
        ocean until
we find the parents who are about to get their script from
        motions of the galaxy and about to
        make love which creates us;
this dim May morning I walk by wet magnolia blossoms
        and the simple wet truth of forsythia.

CONSIDER THE CARD PLAYERS
BY CÉZANNE AS MUSICIAN-SAGES

What's all this craziness that's been going on for centuries
        about the Superman !—in Nietzsche,
                        in Dostoyevsky,
        all that thrashing of self-hatred !?

all this expensive frantic sick advertising of Supersuds,
Superhighways, super-blandness, nullity, mass-murder.
I had uncles playing cards
            in Italy
            at night by grapevines

            and with friends, near fireflies,
who argued a little,
            Uncle Achilles for Instance,
            Zio Antonio per carità ! but this world
            (sometimes with the Madonna and God included)
was enough during those beautiful nights and days
            in Northern Italy.

MIO DIO ! SIAMO ARRIVATI !

Going through all these little drab towns in Maine and New Hampshire
and Massachusetts (a little hard to pronounce by old Italians)
        we
pass this Pizza House or that Pizza Heaven or that Sam's
Pizza or that Leaning Tower of Pizza or that Pizza that surpasseth
        Understanding
and my gods, Columbus, Garibaldi, Volta, Vespucci, Marconi,
        Caruso, we didn't know
what we were Coming To ! but eat your pie and sing !
        Paolo Revere of Boston also
        I was told once was Italian.
A million lovers of all ages gather around a
        huge Pizza and Sing.

I CAN'T STOP FROM BEING SHAKEN,
NEITHER CAN YOU

I am my own goldenrod, I am my own field
I feel as if the wheat is growing in me or at least
that we're going at it together, the sun in the sunflower
and the seeds, all of them with Hindu scripture inside,
just waiting for you to get the right ragas, chants are

141

multiplied like fire burning all of the cities and there is
Shiva, he becomes the goldenrod, he becomes the
dazzling field swaying.

THE SEEDS IN THE SUNFLOWER BECOME
THE BLACK DANCERS IN THE FLAME

Have you been extended like lightning
or like a vine that keeps growing and growing and growing
and growing or like a bean stalk that rises higher and higher
        until Jack is in heaven beating a drum
or like the Ravi Shankar ragas that keep ascending and
        ascending until the universes that are
        meant to be in audience to each seed
        and need begin to dance like
        painted Sanskrit dervishes ?

YOU'RE AWFULLY CLOSE!

There is much remoteness in people

and perhaps our attempt to reach the Moon or Venus
is an attempt to reach them

I or they at times seem to live in a far country
as if we have never left the Realm of Essences
and that suggests our essential need to travel

the sperm or astronaut preparing and restless
goes about its ingenuity and continuity

there is much remoteness in people

when we hear some music or feel it's love
at first sight or third or millioneth sight
we have the notion we're getting in orbit

we're getting there; but as Dante said and Meister Eckhart
there is here; pictures that we make
of distant places illuminate our faces

NOT ALONE IN THE TREMULOUS AND
TRAVELLING SOLAR SYSTEM

As they approach
to put the feet on the Moon
the white and green chairs in the garden tremble

more molecules make Greek drama
and Cassandra and Agamemnon speak
the day lilies of the moment have dew

and blood, the mist is ten centuries old
and today's and momentary, the man
in his Dream, the Armstrong in his machine

approaches the Moon and the crickets in the
garden leap, Christ weeps again knowing
that brother will murder brother

and that man with all his buildings
and computers and ladders that lead up or
down to the Moon has not learned more about love;

the earth trembles, the woman giving birth
dreams of the astronaut her son and father with the flower;
the representative with his delicate foot touches the trembling Moon

PLACE THAT I WILL BE DESCENDING TO,
THAT I WILL BE ASCENDING TO

For me—stranger than the moon, more familiar, place
        I descended to and
ascended to 46 years ago, who knows exactly how, howling my first
        needs, mythologies,

seeing the servants of the seasons come and go like priests,
          people at a country fair, parents,
I keep touching your surface, Mystery, Progenitor, Propagandist
          that I understand, that I stand above,
touching—step by step—sometimes even via iambic
          pentameter,
more distant, near, stranger than stars, more familiar,
          mine, yours,
          Homer's, Chekov's,
world—sacred;   look that you who return from the moon or
          your dream or New Jersey
that you sacred touch upon it lightly saying "I protect you"
          "I imagine you"   "I love you—*earth*."

LIGHT INTO HER

do come
make the sky dance
lead it as if it were a blue bear
with sun oranges to juggle on its nose;
there is Pavlova high on her toes
and then she keeps getting
taller like
champagne
or like
a flag unfurled in the song
the sea has been gathered into a round paper ball
and is being tossed from one child to another
heaven is wild about you
come home again
with me
winner

*

let a clown
lecture to a storm and see what flowers will come out of its
          clouds, crowds will gather to be

dazzled with drizzle; it makes
not a little sense to expect
great downpourings from poetry
and great uprisings from
daisies and audiences;
a girl on a bicycle in the rain followed by a clown
resembling Marcel Marceau
and Chuang-tzu
smiled so that Midi was everywhere; merci beaucoup

INITIATION RIGHTS

Can the poem
enter the sperm and be a sporting Krishna ?
can it enter your most strange and joyous dreams
as different kinds of heroes,
samurai, somersaulter, wayward pitcher, can it
be the cargo of a pitching boat ?
can it come on Stage and Sing ? can it enter
the gold of the darkness
of a bee and be the sounding
of Being ? can it be like
music that comes from the sea ? can it be
instinct which keeps you and me
together ? can it be what relates
star and lover, Quixote and Dulcinea ?
can it be the recognition of Awareness ?
can it be the worthy companion of the Air ?
You won't forget we promised each other Everything.

WE SAY HEROIC AND THE BIRDS ARE BEGINNING TO RETURN, ALMOST APRIL

To arrange the plants by the window is epical enough
to begin with
to watch them grow with their wide leaves and heart shaped
songs and ever continuing expansive vines
is lyrical enough all along

145

to be shaded by them is richness worthy of vibrations,
          celebrations in changing light
will exchange our names; the anonymous reader is married
          to light and dark;
it is a dramatic affair worthy of the Plays of Shakespeare.

THE RECREATION OF EDEN'S SUMMER WHEN COSMIC LOVE DEMANDS IT

Feeling sticky and gooey like those insects coming out
          of cocoons
or like those early buds about to announce to every
          desire
in our living soul that it is Spring on a Sunday
          afternoon
slowly slowly after a luxurious long time
          love making
appealing to all the senses as they say in poetry
          handbooks
revealing all the mysterious buzzing as they say
          in the metaphysics of biology
richly slowly while amazement sits like Tiepolo
          or Antony and Cleopatra dreaming
of us in darkness and emotion, motion, we are
          luminous like wet leaves.

COULD ADAM AND EVE HAVE KNOWN BETTER ?

Am I growing as much as that vine ?
I admire it and see it grow; are some invisible gods
          (maybe with seen vines in their hair ?)
admiring me and viewing me greenly as much as to realize
          that I am like a vine ?
are my days and poems like those growing leaves at my
          window sill now in a moving
          smattering of light and shade ?
each one shiny and formal and perfect, a form of praise;
          I raise the question partly to

climb towards you,
because you see me in a lovely way as
    this poem sees you, you
    the bright one, you
    the perfect one.

WOMEN CARRYING PEACHES

Heaven certainly has its way with fruit
        and women,
look by the French river a beauty is
        carrying beauty,
to behold is to prepare to enter paradise.
O taste and see, sing for the particular
        ineffable unique color form
        of the peach. Of the person.
        Of the moment.
Of what by all together in love is
        pronounced the
        sacred world.

NEVER WITH MACHINERY HAVE WE DONE IT

When
I
landed
on   that
the   moonlight
moon   had
I   been
was   in
so   our
light   music
you   all
were   along
so
enlightened
that

we
knew

FOUR VEGETABLE POEMS

1.
THEY SAY IT IMPROVES
THE EYESIGHT

Some
hidden
orange elf
in the ground,
cozy, snug,
earthy ambitious,
rooted; where
ever you received
the god of your color,
carrot, seeing you
makes our life
bright more vivid.

2.
REGINA STRAORDINARIA

Melanzana
more exotic than
Melanesian, purple,
glowing very glowing
very glowing, how can
I be exotic Enough to have
a true rapport with you ?

3.
THE VINE DIVINE

I had a
thin exquisite
tall young cousin,
something about her

delicacy, shape,
slightly greenish
color, north Italian,
slightly Mona Lisa smile,
makes me think of her in
connection with Leonardo
and string beans; not
having praised them Enough
now I'm pleased to
divine this connection.

4.

PEAS SAID THE GARDEN
AND PLEASED WE WERE

peas
perfect peas
green small and large
perfect green peas
related to Mistress Green
and the Green Queen her mother
and the 12 comedies of my puppet plays
in which they are mentioned; fields
of coolness; pea pods of coolness;
perfect piselli pleasing piselli
excellent and cool petit pois and
blissful beholders of all these green peas

FORTUNATELY TOMATOES

THE PASTORAL READER EXACTLY PREPARING

Look
red cardinal
your religion tells you to get close to the
        tomato plants,
they're growing (the tomatoes) like churches in the best of
        times for churches,
the leaves at least if not the envy of angels the accompaniment
        in green perfection
of angels and Eden and tomatoes, cardinal, your redness sumptuous

exact if not the envy of lovers
        the accompaniment of their
Eden and perfection and tomatoes; somebody in the garden
        is ready to notice.

THE FIELDS OF VEGETABLES-AND-LITERATURE DRENCHED

What happened when the rivers humidly and invisibly
        entered the sky
and then came down like so many noisy
        thick rivers ?
were the Shinto priests preparing to shake their leaves
        under a temple roof
or adolescent poets beginning to write were having their
        first emissions ?
surprised they took it upon themselves to utter words
        like wet and I bet you
        the gods are envious;
the summer world is receiving its fulfillment, the
        tomatoes are doused, the vines like
        the thoughts of Shakespeare
        are responding to
        THE TEMPEST.

ABUNDANCE
and imagine when you press Them ! when you bite Them !

They seem supernatural
but what could be more natural !
they are glowing, they are huge very huge luscious bright
        shining red very red very red,
large to put it mildly, full juicy sumptuous the
        summa theologica of vegetable summer,
brought over, about 7 of them, mellow, magnificent, as
        if from another world, and
yet they came out of the earth just as they say Adam and
        Eve did, but these are
so immediate so appetizing so holdable, when glories
        become sensuous as these
then Nature in what seems her most operatic and supernatural

Mode can pronounce
TOMATOES.

A FUTURE ITALIAN ENVISIONS THE MIRACLES

The last tomatoes have been taken from the vines, the sticks
      upholding them have been pulled out
      of the wet ground,
the cold air is bright and the frost is coming tonight
      or soon;
from something before seed I'll call it song to bud to
      green fruit, red fruit, lovely
      to see, lovely to hold,
good to eat; and so now more than several dozens of those tomatoes
      have become part of my green and red song.
But out there in the field they are gone and
      winter is coming.
The birds are in migration. Dreams are taking directions.
      Soil, soul, sun,
be patient, be active preparing your prayers
      envision green then red
      the future *pomodori*.

OPUS ONE AND OPUS TWO AND
OPUS THREE:IN PRAISE OF CABBAGES

AUTUMNAL HIM, HEAVY WEIGHT OF PRAISE

how large a cabbage
did the cabbage grow larger
shall we put the world in the cabbage
and say O boy what a vegetable ! shall we
praise the Word for such cabbages and include
the weather   shall we grow in praise as the Cabbage
is Noticed   shall we not praise the God of all Cabbages
for designs and greenery   shall we not welcome the farmers
      who remember all cabbages   shall not all
cabbages be grandparents and godparents and those who favor the
      Green density and opulence of metaphysics ?
godsons in green glory give THANKSGIVING to Cabbages.

I AM AMAZED THAT SO HEAVY A MAGNIFICENCE
COULD HAVE SUCH DELICATE ROOTS   I CHEER
FOR IT;   OCTOBER

is That That the Very Earth Itself
or God Disguised as the Autumn *Hugest God of Green
          Cabbages*—
le chou ? my friend the poet and ecologist Bob Chute
          extravagantly again
marvellously wowed me by giving us a most to say the least
          Stupendous Cabbage
I figure it includes Falstaff and the Globe I figure that
          theologians as green freshmen
          within are miniscule talking about God
          within its theatrical heavy strong Green Leaves
it will take days or months of ingenuity by my cooking Grace
          to make cabbage preparations for my
          Gargantuan appetite, I'm small
compared to It, like Puck; is Chute descendent of *chou* or
          is *chou* descendent of Chute ?
descending from the poetic skies in green parachutes
          elves appeared on the farm and pleased by
          vegetables vegetables began a
          Cabbage Celebration !

THE ECOLOGIST CALMLY RENDERS ANOTHER SURPRISE

Petit Chou
dear little cabbage
green head I touch you
small as you are you are as mystic and magnificent
          as any song can be,
freshness is contained in you and future strength; I
          play Prospero by your
          calmness and I
ask your blessings in return. The World which is no
          better or worse than a cabbage
          or its symphony yearns
          for our Meeting.
The Sun our Relative prospers warmth, a blessing,
          poetry as something seen,
          tasted. So now that
we've made this 3rd Cabbage Opera, this vegetable ritual, I
          render thanks to those

mysterious gift givers
Bob and Vicki Chute.

****

The 1st Cabbage was given to me a few years ago just before Thanksgiving and the 2nd, even larger, was given to me the following October; the poems were written on these Rabelaisian Occasions immediately after the Enormous Gifts were Received; the Gifts were from Bob Chute, Farmer Poet Friend. The presentation of a more diminutive (but not less Valuable) cabbage led to the writing recently of OPUS THREE.

MORE VEGETABLES AND GENEROSITY

FOR YEARS, MANY, I'VE SUCCUMBED TO THEM

Now a potato can be a Willendorf Venus,
         all bumpy,
Bulky, earth mother as the professorial
         mythology books say,
I prefer potatoes (to the professorial
         abstractions I mean)
bumpy, huge, with delicate skins,
         of the earth, and yet
related to sky, sun, rain, and to the genius
         of all vegetables,
these enormous, at times hippopotamus like,
         mind-boggling shapes
have much to do with nourishment, substantiality,
         and organic poetry.
Wittgenstein and the Willendorf Venus are making out.

ONCE MORE THE VEGETABLES ARE PRONOUNCED

Piece of spinach
growing asserting your strong delicate unique
         individuality, that as praise to
         God and presentation of your
         Self,
Peace of spinach
         in the huge wandering universe, with its chaos,

wars,
        galaxies, gods, coming and going,
the thought of you
        at the moment
        gives me strength.

LETTUCE DOES NOT LET US ALONE

A green plot, or chlorophyll scheme, terrestrial
        intrigue, vegetables
asserting themselves, my vegetables having their say,
        characters
in a mystery play could not be more religious,
        we are each others'
        symbolists,
grass, fish, stars, actors in a Shakespeare Play,
        exclamations in a
        Hopkins' poem,
rabbits, Easter ceremonies, the Seasonal Director
        unseen is as wise
        as can be, we
sometimes forget our parts, sometimes forget our lines,
        then Thoreau is critical,
        then all the best
poems from every where are helpful. Birds and the
        theater of air and light.
Having a Sunday to think, co-operating we
        made the world again.

SNIFFING, MUNCHING,   AND AS THEY LIKE IT

Celery, Celery, Cecelia's disguise, green peas nearby,
        cool, a little wet,
a little wedding wouldn't do us any harm, forget me nots,
        tiny violets, dawn, faun, dew,
back to back, toes cool, streams nearby, trickles,
        tiny leaves brush against the
        naked bodies of
the waking ones, I'm hungry he said, she also was.
        They were as light as could be
        as giddy as youth
could be in Springtime or any pretty ring time as they
        were having pretending easily

they were rabbits celery
for busy breakfast.

ANOTHER VEGETABLE OCCASION
TO THANK THE CHUTES

Ah, summer squash, light yellow, curved,
        bumpy, luminous,
delectable, edible, an event to be
        radiant about, increasing
desire, appetite, summer friendship.
        Summer squash, summer squash.

"A FASCINATING ACCOUNT OF THE PHYSICAL, EMOTIONAL, AND SPIRITUAL RELATIONS BETWEEN PLANTS AND MAN" *THE SECRET LIFE OF PLANTS* by Peter Tompkins and Christopher Bird

It takes some choosing, one must have a green thumb, one must
        have the grace of God, it takes
a lot of Mysterious pushing, humorous persistency, and
        directing one's body-and-soul and daily
        gestures and plans to "l'amor che move
        il sole e l'altre stelle",
it takes a long constant very dramatic long often
        bewildering sometimes exhausting really
        tremendous struggle to spiritually
        survive, to reflect
transcendent harmonies and choreography in one's relationship
        with plant, tree, any object (with its
        musical messages), wife (with her needs,
        demands), children (with their
        mysteries and children
        and everyone
in the complete cosmic meaningful Commotion)
        it takes all the help we can get
        from the secret life of plants,
        from the secret life of saints,
        from the secret-and-public life
        of the best lovers and poems.

155

And there as if an Egyptian god
had suddenly reared itself on the Florida asphalt
on the road from Crescent Lake to St. Augustine a strange oracle
a white mouthed moccasin, poisonous they say as all get out,
and beautiful as man, artist, mystery,
   put up its head
and we in a car made of junk, tin, factory, we with
   college notes and literature
and history stopped to admire the pre-historic priest
   archaic
   stunning
   a very speaking part of Osiris
and from a distance as a theologian is from a distance admiring
   his dream of God
we looked and Bob Chute like a saint who knew somewhat his
   biology, his own I mean and maybe
a little about the snake and its ancestors and the hand that
touched
   its belly Into Creation,
he, my friend (I hope to include the Snake but now I mean my
   colleague)
poked him (the Mystery, the Perfect) and told him to escape unto
   his hiding, freedom or some such human Word,

and like a rippling of darkness
like a stream of black flying quickly the one who held up
   tin and junk civilization
uniquely inimitably rippled into the distances of the
   cool grass.

As a bit of social criticism let me add some fierce Florida
   dolled up women with glasses
   and probably guns somewhere and insurance policies
   harsh voices white faces
   and blotch of thin red for lips
   and a brand new car like a shined up
   dead husband
saw Chute (as if descended from a Northern parachute) and the
   college girls and boys and me
   Romantic about the fellow Mystery
and harshly they said as if they were in Pop Art or ready to
   run our hands over with their brand new car
   or their brand of "power"

"Kill that Snake" "run over it with your goddam car"
        but

we were out for Beauty and we startled Him into Where He
        Came From
And the Daughters of Motels and we lovers of Thoreau
        and stars and America
        gloriously went our
        Separate Ways.

TO LEARN TO COMMUNICATE IS TO BE ORIGINAL, TO RE-CREATE GENESIS

Stars are born, whales are born, fleas are born.
        And then die.
The great ooze of Zeus, the flux of foam and oceans and
        sliding cliffs.
And a small bird flies over the Atlantic and finds its
        "home." A word feels
        good in this place.
Stand on your head. Admire Marcel Marceau. Tell Pascal
        we know how to tremble.
A hand of a dead sailor comes up from the sea. A child
        waves goodbye to its mother.
        The leaves of grass blow in
        the great prairie wind.
The stars sweep over the ship of the particular sailor,
        every one unique
        every one related.
And lonely. And merging. And finding the sea shell under
which
        is the magic alphabet.
It is Noah's Ark all wet.

        An angel announces the
        death of a flower, the
        birth of a word.

IN ANY TIME—IT IS AN ARK—
IT IS A COVENANT—IT IS A SYMPHONY

To dedicate a Library
        take all the students of the world
        and know their needs. I know
        they need Montaigne, I know they
        need Mt. David, Socrates, Rabelais,
        Bhagavad-Gita, old and new testaments,
        Mozart, Monet; and here in the Library
        the International sit-in prospers, Spinoza
        next to Prospero, e.e. cummings next to Dante,
        here the love-in is wordy, is singing;
To dedicate a Library
        take all the teachers of the world
        and see them bowing to the Word
        and all the students. And know their
        needs. I know they need to be
        beginning students always. Plays,
        Prayers, Poems.
To dedicate a Library
        take all the modesty and all the mysteries
        and all the needs and songs born and yet to
        be born of all the people and trust them,
        entrust your life to generosity, give your
        books to friends, known, unknown;
To dedicate a Library
        take courage, take heart,
        give all your passion and your comedy,
        see all the children of all ages
        in need of magic, in need of
        metaphors, the trees,
the great trees, the great leaves of grass, the great
        books, the looks of lovers improve
        as they see the dove;
To dedicate a Library honor and
        know the destiny of Noah.

        (for the 1979 Dedication
        of the George and Helen Ladd
        Library at Bates College)

GUARDIANS OF THE FAITH

To guard the works of art—
my gods, what lions we have to be !
to guard in a golden way the lines of poetry
how we must roar bravely and poetically !
to really regard our gods and words and
works of art what splendid lions we become !

THE PROOF IS IN THE BEAUTY
OF THE INDIVIDUALS

What am I doing for my country ?
I am keeping myself in tact,
I am feeling it up, reality, really
     I want to smell it, I want
     to feel its wetness, I want
     my body to be as fresh as if
     I came out of a shower or a
     bath or the Womb Itself
     to be with It, as a child
     is by the breast, as a swimmer
     is with the water or brilliant air,
     or a musician deep in the thought
     of his very music; I want to
     feel the pear, eat it, touch
     the bark of the tree, sniff the
     coming of autumn, announce
     the dazzling advent of winter,
     be as elemental as a polar bear,
     as intimate as an experienced husband;
United Nations, what am I doing for you ?
we are keeping ourself in tact, me, my wife,
     my children, my responsive lyrical
     students; you can look at them

     and see how beautiful this
     political generosity can be.

SHE COMES WITH HER ARMS FULL
OF LILACS AND FUGUES PROCEED

To come to Sumptuous thoughts, Brahms, Wallace Stevens,
    Connoisseur of Symphonies and Splendors

of Symbols, sunsets and the birth of any insect, leaf,
            plant, poem,
to venture the plays of Shakespeare, to project the stars
            of the most precise
telescope, to tell Toscanini to continue conducting,
            to summarize all wet the discoveries of
            Jacques Cousteau, to reveal Ravel,
to unbutton Bach, to release the music so that the
            bravest and most modest Bates student
will proceed, graduate towards Summer with his arms full
            of future books, with his songs
            light with future airiness,
with devotion to his love, to come to Sumptuous thoughts,
            those harmonies that made your parents and
            the planets 1st wildly insistently
            demand you, tells of Eden,
tells of Commencements, more symphonies and babies and ducks and
            epics born in the Eternal Now.

                              *

                    Inside the Sunflower
                    is the Sun inside
                    the Sun is Blake
                    writing about the
                    Sunflower in the Sun.

HIGHEST HONORS;   COOLNESS,   BREEZE

To have a slightly moving green house
kissed by rain
in slightly moving light or shade always new
and to be able to fly to another slightly moving
green house in different kinds of weather amidst
different kinds of songs
is prerogative of birds
privilege of words.

AFTER SCHOOL

A poet winds himself up into exhilaration—
    it's voice training !
    by giving lectures, it's like
        going up a beautiful cliff,
    and then looks at the sea,
        then late at night sitting high
up there he sends poems, he lets
    them fall
    like pollen out of an unknown flower.

LIKE SHAKESPEARE ABOUT TO WRITE
THE 1ST LINE OF THE 1ST PLAY

Think of all the
    agitation
    moods *etc.* that went into the writing of the
    words in all those many books lined up there on
    the long shelves facing me and all I have to do
    provided the impulse is somewhat awake in me is to
    take one from the shelf wondering and open it and God knows
        what will happen, there's
    Faulkner for instance—and Conrad—and St. Augustine—
        and Chekov—
    Blake and Shelley—can you imagine all that
        commotion in there and they
        seem so quiet—
I have to make my choices—now they are not
        afraid, now they are immortal,
    I somewhat shake, I move my hand towards one,
        soon the performance to be continued
        will begin.

MY AMBITION GROWS

While reading Marianne Moore, while thinking of you,
    my ambition grows, I have the
    dictionary near me
I would like to write a poem about every word
    in the dictionary,
Later . . . I thought also most animals. Not all
    works of art, but many all over
    the world.

161

Desires make me feel as if I already had
            helicopters. As if you and I could
            fly around over Central Park.
            Land wherever you want,
            love.

ONE LEAPING DOLPHIN REGARDING
ANOTHER, ETC. . . . ETC. . . .

The music keeps making the shade go up
you can't be secretive
whatever you've got it will show in the universe
whatever the universe has got it will show in you
you don't even have to be intentional
or what used to be called educated
what you've got to do is be born
and that happens as often as it's
necessary for you; some seem luckier,
some seem lovelier, but grace like all
the fish in the sea forever and ever is
something in motion, music, and apparent.

THE DIVINITY SCHOOL ADDRESS

One doesn't have to continue to paint portraits of
            one's self in order to
make self-portraits, any object will do, old shoes,
            starry night, sun flower;
you think of Van Gogh, I started by seeing a vast bulky
            magnificent golden Rembrandt
            self-portrait;
style is the man; turn to Emerson and Turner for
            intensive expanding ecstasy.

rhythm
like a horse
was taking him far, where ? ah, what a lovely night, how cool and
        lovely, see the stars, see the moon,
he rode by darkness in darkness
        in joy with joy
        in love by love
        O he knew the way to the Holy Cities
he was going
        at different speeds
        beautiful beautiful that horse
        sometimes galloping
        sometimes walking slowly
        sometimes sleeping
        his head rich with music
sometimes going very fast
        walking slowly
        now through a dazzling town
        the minarets uttered prayers
        the minutes celebrated
this is the most prosperous and peaceful time in the
        village and lovers
        who know so much
        are beginning to recite poetry

THE LEAPING WISH OF THE SAINT BECOMES TRUE

Intelligence. Intuition into It,
        into the circles of stones where
        the ancient cricket with the face of a god
        prays, into
the empty room that is moving slowly where the
        student will begin to pronounce
        Plato; and then Peter;

perfection will blossom like the breeze made by an angel's
    wings, wherever the lovers go their shadows
    will make
the stones begin to sing; the stream is persistent, flourishes
    like God's prophecy, the multi-
    religioned fish in it
are heard to speak strange stories wet with rainbow action,
    they leap, we sleep,
heard to murmur mighty sentences like the one who found
    a key in the mouth of a fish.

WE PICTURE YOUR MIGRATION

Who am I
drifting here amidst, late at night, the words of a
    thousand books,
stars and the beginnings of sleep, drifting as sea weed
    or galaxy
slowly, and yet the current is felt, like sea air,
    not thinking of reaching
    any place and yet
with a sense of direction as palpable as the breath within
    these poems;
there is the space within the dreams of the animals
    and I signal to it,
my brothers at the conclave at Altamira respond
    making pictures on the wall.

LET THE WORLD GO

let it go out of your hand like a ball thrown like a bird flying
you'll be surprised to see it always turning like a musician always
    returning like God to admire man
you'll be amazed by flying festivals, dragons will be like
    grammarians by comparison,
you'll be surprised to see how large the world is what a spinning
    concert singing to you it is.
Why don't the chairs fly off ? why don't the words fly off the
    page ? sometimes they do.

Do you know that two lovers on that world are not forgetting
    you ?
You whose center is everywhere and whose circumference is
    mentioned by a poem.
The notes of musicians made astrologers of us.
The notes of children learning how to write recalled the
    fabled Word.

AS I WATCH MY GROWING DAUGHTERS

Do you know why the beautiful world trembles ? I do. I like it
        that way in the heaven of air, in the
        dalliance of music that surrounds us
        and the Muse of every object. It is
because we are delicate and insistent and infinitely vibrant and
        persistent and demanding and therefore
        tremulous and because of this strong
        and thank God lyrical and epic and dramatic
in our relationships; it is because of this. Keats knew. And
        Monet too. But also essentially and eventually
        all others. Do you know (moving
        as can be with the world and other stars)
why the beautiful Word trembles ?   we do.

WHY ARE YOU EVERY WHERE ?
WELL, I'M NOT COMPLAINING

Does any one mail more mail than I do ?
I don't think so; not even Sears Roebuck,
not even seals spouting on their way to one
of their favorite really pleasurable resorts do,
I send out poems to you and you and you at times
momentously; when rainbows are in the spray
of dolphins many many many dolphins as many
as there are readers then I have the splashy feeling
you are saying thank you in all the languages of
        human generosity.
Coming and going, under the moon, under the sun, we

surrender everything
to each other.

NOT TIED DOWN

One is tied up to one's god—Apollo or Dionysus or
               Aquarius or Sagittarius—
and he in his space ship made of balloons
                   or poems
                   or fireworks

        takes you for a ride

near what Plato called the Doctrine of Ideas
or what Jung called the fables at the bottom of the sea

        Can you change
        your god in mid air ?

        Can you change
        your Pegasus in mid stream

        I dreamt commissioned by Wu Ch'eng-en that I was a
monkey and could

THE OPERATIC AUDIENCE IS GETTING READY

    Often
    I feel like dancing naked—
    is not that the sign of the spirit ?

    the universe is dancing naked and brilliant
    next to another universe naked and brilliant
    next to another universe naked and brilliant
    and so on for many light years
    as they energetically send
    each other messages,

songs:

if Someone's Watching that's His Business

IN A GREEN WORD THE GODS
BUILD THEIR TRAVELLING HOMES

You turn into water but
then you always turn back into yourself
you turn into cloud and into skies where we drifted
        like young balmy lovers and joked
and lounged and laughed and rested naked so that Greek art
        began where our shadows sang
you turned into a Spring tree with surprising flowers you turned
        into a sleepy dancer with mouths
that wounded like arrows of bees you turned into a bush
        with insects working
you turned into a smooth stream where I slipped like a
        perfect fish
you turned into a jewel from which I looked like a blazing
        dreamer
you turned into a sticky stick with thick buds and I within
        the compressed wood
kissed as if by pressing unknowns burned like a delirious
        dancer
or like a star at the tip of a wand you turned into a
        wandering you
and I sought you all over the world.

SLIGHTLY ABOVE THE DANCE FLOOR THE GODS
AND GODDESSES MEET NEAR ACCORDIANS

When the music uplifts the dancers
as if it were related to the power of Spring to make
        the flowers rise
and from the divine ground the sleepers suddenly have
        their fling

and sing to each others arms no harms come to the
        whirling world
but all charms; all of a sudden a Greek band
        jangling in the dark
summons Dionysus and summer and students; stars
        join in and tell
the musicians about the music of the spheres; from
        one hint to another, from
        one hand to another,
the crowd Swaying tells the moving center we have
        an order to shake wildly
        and propagate peace.

SAUNTER FOREVER O DOLPHINS MYTHOLOGICALLY DREAMING OF US

        At the middle of the heights of our love life
I had so many noisy sendings of wetness, juice, joy,
        expirations, romantic gasps
that the night might be thinking a series of dolphins was
        explosively partaking of the divine,
fireworks in the soft flower night, wet; Joyce at the
        pub, boisterous Dylan, blazing
        Blake, could not be more
splurging sonorous. Little lambs on green pastoral hills
        by Angelic capitals and mossy Cathedrals
and the smell of haystacks and farms and French bread
        could not be more glowing Arcadian.
Look, Proteus is procreating Again. Barnacle Bill is
        snoring. Some sumptuous readers
dizzy dazzled utterly drizzled drenched are ready to
        touch the thigh of the Shaking Wonder
        of Words-in-Water.

a bee grew very large it must have been God because it reached the flower
a woman grew very large she must have been the mother of God because
    she had a baby
a baby grew very large he must have been the sky because he
    contained many moods and thoughts
a Thought grew very large it must have been God because it
    contained all weddings and religions
a celebration grew very large it must have been the descendants
    of rainbows
because everybody was in the sun
the sun grew very large it must have been the Word
    from which God was imagined
the image grew very large it must have been mankind
    because it was amidst all stars

BURNING   BRIGHT

I looked   up
and I saw   a   tiger   it was only made of paper
but what was the paper made of   and what were its colors made of ?
and what were the trees that
                made the paper
                related to and
                what about the painter in the
factory who painted
        this job
        this orange   and green   and white   paper tiger mask ?
        evidently
it was marvellous in its own way
                since
                an artist
free and earning money for his pussy cat had a hand in it
and what was it
                Vivekananda said ?
                I look up
the Quotation:
                "If you cannot see God in the human face, how can you
                see Him in clouds, etc. ? When you see man as God,

God, everything, even the tiger will become welcome."

I look up

and there   was

VIVEKANANDA,
vivid, orange,   growling like a tiger

YOU

Deck out
                the Decalogue
said the tipsy Captain to the Scrubbing Sailors;
the waves insisted on knocking them down;
the air insisted on caressing them and singing
        to them,
the fish insisted on nibbling at them like dreams,
the Magna Carta and the Carta Geographica and the
        Magnet Wheel
insisted on following them, so everytime they came up
        spouting
they were all nationalistic, humanistic and above all
Transcendental Misfits. Their fitful dancing late
        at night
on the Waters of the World like the Belly of Creation
aroused Gossip. Theologians predicted. But when they
        Returned Home
with Mermaids or Pearls or Treasures in their High Hands
        they became the Rulers
that are now seen sitting on any Cliff like the
        Title above a Poem.

ON BEING ASKED FOR A ROUGH DRAFT

Rough
        rough
            draft
            windy day
            blowing poems

around in the museum
which was like Noah's ark on fire
held by the desire of angels, golden
Golden was the event; rougher and rougher
the weather grew and as librarians got their
books out, their spectacles out, their other
      tools of learning out
the fish leapt between the words; rainbows
      covered the bibliography;
weather men weathered it; the compass
      crowed; the wet singer crooned;
the moon was musical over the
      calmer sea. The musician hit a
      high C. The prima donna hit a
      musician. The audience applauded
      wildly. As that happened the copy got
      rougher and rougher until a Captain
      with a million fish hanging out
      smelling salty as creation
      talked about Creative Writing Courses
      and those who registered
      won all the prizes
      including the nameless ones.
Once is not more than enough;
Rougher and rougher and rougher and rougher
etc. the weather and captains grew *etc.*

COLOMBIAN WHISTLES IN BIRD FORMS

High in the mountains
in Colombia somebody was
whistling, the person in love
wandering was whistling in
any country, all the tunes
have easily migrated like
perfect birds to where the
1st Sound of Love made
them and the active lovers Necessary.
The perfect lovers knowing how to fly
towards each other are resounding in
      Colombia.

The boat on the river of eternity was very long
    longer than you can think,
    longer than you can say,
but everybody's song will accompany it, so listen
    all the time to when the dead
    and the living and all relatives
including the beaver, the mink, the muskrat, the giant bear,
    the salmon, the birds, all
the voices in the dreams and the winds are definitely arriving;
    children arrive in the Museum of Natural History
    here in NYC, Chinese, Africans, Americans
    of all colors, originators of all myths
and they are sort of debonair and gaping as they stare silently
    or variously chatter and laugh
    as they circulate, following their teacher who holds a flag in
    the air, the very long Northwestern canoe.
The noise of the cascades, the noise of all ancestral voices,
    the undulating noise of the very amused children
all keep us very entertained as we watch the undescribable long voyage
    of the very long decorated canoe on the river eternity.

THE RELIGIOUS DANCER IS
TREMENDOUSLY APPARENT

    If you ask where he is hiding I will say in
        the belly of a fish
    I will say in the wind over the stream
    I will say in the motion of the grass
    I will say in the swaying of the dancers
    I will say in the sound of your stomping
    I will say in the words within the words of your prayers
    I will say in the fire in every home
    I will say in the light under the wing of a bee
    I will say in the head of a dew filled flower
    I will say in the grace of any animal
    I will say in the imagination of the prophet
        why do you say
    he is hiding when we all see him everywhere
        do you want

to keep him all for yourself ? it is you who are
hiding the complete sensual body of
the apparent, Krishna Himself,
when you say we do not see Him in Dazzling Action Everywhere.

ANTHROPOLOGICAL SONG, ANCIENT AND RECENT

Like a primitive person I must follow my prayer wherever it goes,
if it sails through a rainbow I will be there,
if it eats with the grasshopper I will be there,
if it is a flute song I will be air,
if it is a shadow I will be its dance,
I cannot let it get away from me
otherwise we would die.

I DRINK TO YOUR LONG LIFE, O POEM

Is that the "conclusion" I derived, that I climbed to, that
the higher the mountains are the
longer we live ?
that was in a color movie about longevity, about old old people
climbing mountains daily, companions
to goats and cold rivers, bathing in
the early morning coldness, naked,
by flowers, in those fast streams;
I love long beards
and some, over 100 years old, had curly hair dyed red;
and some drank and danced
an awful lot; I wish to
join them finding monasteries, finding white bearded goats,
finding strange tastes in distant festivals,
finding a new flower after
age 140,
after spitting and laughing and dancing like a little demon
with the wind.

173

Two pigeons
wondering
what to do
one Sunday
afternoon,
very gray,
it had
snowed
for months
in Maine,
one sat on
one branch,
another on
a branch below,
just looked
around the
provinces

where it was
going to snow
again. They
kept moving
their heads,
like philosophers
or old ladies,
had their
picture taken
by this dim
poem and then
they disappeared
for a while.

*

There
is
an
invisible
bridge
sometimes
you
want
to
call
it
light
sometimes
you
want
to
call
it
darkness

we
know
there
is
an
invisible
bridge.

JUST A FEW SCENES FROM
AN AUTOBIOGRAPHY

I eat noodles with the Emperor's brother
in a school basement, he tells me about baseball,
I tell him about Gagaku

I translate the sounds of a cricket
with a musician or elf then
I become the cricket

I go to the moon with my mother
and we weep there for all the ashes
and for all the dead in all the wars

I look at student essays by the millions
and put scribbles meaning awkward near some words
I prepare lectures for over 30 years

I listen to messages from all things that
sooner or later are speaking directly to me
and my wife and I travel in love

DEBUSSY AND PROUST

The Customs Seal on my travel bag
          almost faded,
          looking like a miniature of an old map,
the old vaccination mark on my left arm almost faded,
          the dim moon in the morning sky,
          the memory of so many days
          and nights and flowers come
          and gone almost faded;
before you go, map of God on the fading body of the dancer,
mark of acceptance by the international officer,
          ancient body of an insect on a leaf,
          before you go I want to just
          mention you, repeat your names,
          say the alphabet from A to Z,
want to say as long as I can remember I will

murmur prayers and the reverence
of things past.

UNDER THE BRIM OF MY SHAKING STRAW HAT

I have often thought about the meaning of limitations—how they
    are the apparent markings of time in the endless Present—
how though after months of sailing around the Cape of Good Hope and
    through the Straits of Gibraltar and in the Indian Ocean
and after nights of feeling the curves of the body of the person we
    love, of tasting the nipple, of feeling the fuzz, of again
    and again searching and sailing, we feel that
there is more to find, and we fragile universe show up
    as we can; it is this hinter land, this transition land
    of hints and ever renewed tokens of taste
and instinct that acknowledges the tale of a comet or the
    migrations of salmon or the repeated
annual moon instructed manual of the gigantic turtles;
    another god is deposited on the sand, and when it
    speaks to the ear of the muse of the poem
centuries before it is written it says this is not all, this
    is not all, this is not the end.

VAST NIGHT BEFORE WINTER

    I see them still not spears but stars
        falling through the skies
    on many August nights but years and years
        ago it seems
    now as tired after tears and no tears, after all
        the thousand
    passionate more or less, mostly more, lectures,
        Henry James today,
    Melville before, then Shakespeare and on and on, the
        stars are falling
    towards hidden and summer rabbits, the waterfalls and
        streams, earth relatives,

all of us relatives—and so we are falling falling
    like stars; who will remember ?

EGYPTIAN RELIEF OF BLIND HARPIST

I can feel the Sun,
I can hear the river flowing by in
    the night
and hear the flowers opening, I can hear
    the birds
as they begin to fly, thousands of them, and
    then I remember
them and the vastness, I can sense the
    water very deep in the
desert, when I touch these strings I can hear
    the soul fly in the sky.

DECEMBER 3RD

How can you come to a
conclusion, Wordsworth
or Anybody ? doesn't the weather
always change ? the snowflakes falling now
are new heavenly rejoiners, each one unique too—
just as no two sonnets are the same just as no two
sounds of O or Ah or anything are the same; the vowel or
        the snowflake seems to disappear;
        it is a brief visitor in Venice or Lewiston,
        give it
your changing kind of courtesies. They are preparing
        mangers
        the sentences;
many magi in all sorts of disguises are wondering what
        To Bring;
Music is giving them hints; when there is a brief visitor
        called an angel
        In A Poem

177

what will you Sing ? Sentences like many people keep going
to a new Nativity Scene.

"TO WRITE POETRY ONE
MUST BE PREPARED TO DIE."
—THEODORE ROETHKE

Ah sacred hands
        that are becoming older
        more like the branches of trees
        more like twigs in winter
        more like the fossils of fish
        more like ancient signals of our evolution
        yet wanting to turn pages of old and new testaments
ah fingers related to monkeys, to active Puck,
        to the electric discharge of universes,
ah tips of fingers feeling and thereby knowing the way to
        crawl, to climb, to touch
        upon all tokens of the
        gifts of relatives,
ah invisible and universal and unique mind and hands
        and all that goes with the body's
        desire always searching and
knowing the way that cannot be described to grasp the Unknown.

IN THE PALMS OF ANCIENT BODHISATTVAS

In due time bridges collapse, handsome people get
        very old looking, call it deterioration,
        old age, erosion,
but look at the Ponte Vecchio, look at Rembrandt's
        self-portraits in old age, cliffs
can be ancient testaments, old Hebrew prophets can
        be mind-boggling in their power, beauty,
the signs of age on a magnificent enormous tree or
        elephant or elaborate Hindu temple
can make a new fluorescent bank look bland, blank.
        There is that rugged Ghirlandaio grandfather

with the bumpy nose; the admiring young Florentine
    grandson knows experience and kindness
    when he sees it;
listen to the old WINTER'S TALE; arrive at the
    breezy condition of taoist old wanderers.
We progress from one mystery to another like ageless
    grasshoppers summoned precisely.

MOVING THE WORDS OF A POEM AS IF
THEY WERE LEAVES OF A GOLDEN BOUGH
OR A NEW GREEN ONE

These acquaintances, these friends, who have already died,
    I wake this morning not quite
    awake, realize my eye-sight
    is getting worse, though it's
a bright day, cold, I think of them as if they were water
    pouring from a cupped hand,
once substantial, unique, with that ineffable local color
    and peculiarity each one had,
and all in utter dialogue with me, we exchanged recognition,
    jokes, moods, moments,
what is a past moment ? rain at the feet of roots, soon it
    will be Shakespeare's birthday,
Spring in Maine and the heart shakes like a morning star.

EARLY DECEMBER

The grandeur of a horse
the grandeur of a horse walking in snow
the grandeur of a house like a horse; the slow horse
    lifting its white head,
shaking its mane like the weather rattled in sun,
    the high Son
like a prince of peace by trees in snow, by
    birds and berries
by ghosts and lakes and housewives cooking, slowly
    this king walks

shaking his head so that the sun quivers and the
    silver lines all over the world shake;
his presence breaks the news of Grandeur to the
    Vast Scene as if
    Life suddenly appeared in the waiting Mind.

THE COMMUNION

What is the sound
that a bear likes to hear when it is dying
    now that it is snowing so hard
or that a fish must hear when it is
    inventing the universe ?
a child walking to school through forests and forests and
    centuries until he comes to the
millennium is repeating to himself those magic phrases
    that made Mozart and Shakespeare begin
    to be expressive; the trees
are very silent, so he can remember, later he looks up
    and sees that the stars were
    working it out for him.
When he arrives at the celebration place where he meets
    everyone he loved in his life
they repeat the sound so that the next traveller all afire with
    Consciousness is determined.

A GIFT BEFORE THE SUN
HIBERNATES IN JANUARY

O Jewelled Day
Great Tree with the Many Arms of Fires
from your walls we perceive the gathering of Light,
Many Elephants Sleeping with Their Heads Towards the Dream,
this Winter Day uplift the Reader Rider Writer, the Jewel
    in His Brow, the Jewel in the Dancing Hands
    of the Day, Fire to Fire, tongue of Flame
    to tongue of Flame. In the vast Tree
    which has been preparing its poems

for many years in a few months
there will be prophets in Green,
Now the Jewel like the Sun
turns mysteriously in the
Seen and Seeing, the Scene
and Death; from the
Darkness
and the Coldness in the limpid Clarity of the Dim Blue
    Moment
meeting the flaming ambassadors; down the corridors
    of the varied colors of Light
    of the Jewel are seen
    Angels Running
    Towards You.

YES, WE CAN STAND ALL THESE NOBEL PRIZES, COMETS, UNIVERSES, EPICS, THEY KEEP COMING OUR WAY

Receiving this grant from
the earth I became a millionaire;
I whiffed the air.

Receiving this grant from
time I made a rime,
we joined the Event;

knowing we had the magic ring,
eventually with "idleness in love"
and Oberon we heard every one

and every thing sing; the body
of the golden dancer called the
First Day keeps pouring it out,

light, more light, all seasons,
all music; eventually with Shakespeare
Dreaming and all named and unnamed poets

moment by moment we were
granted all this
verbal eternity.

*

The evening
is like a plant that is growing
out of the mouths of the dead,
the great leaves rattle their wings in the Width of Mystery,
the patterns on the leaves are the fortunes told by angels,
the roots that go down very deep into the ancestors standing
    below ancestors who are standing
    below other actors
are like the filaments of music . . .
    rampagers on scene
    cavort, sport, do their
    Bugaku, send Ionesco
    for a bicycle ride, see how it is raining raining raining
and the millions of people who are walking or flying in the iridescence
    of the night are using flowers
    for umbrellas, some not
    bothering are just drumming

THE RESTORATION

When it comes to me
I want to hide behind the sun
and then penetrate through it and people will see
    how bright they are
or I want to hide behind the moon
and then appear like a Noh Actor chanting
so that people watching on TV or via telepathy will
    will get it and become lunatics
    lovers poets
or hide behind the cricket and wear its mask so
    that we will leap in
    the fields of summer

or ask you to join me and hide behind every every
      object and then together
      like dazzling engineers
we will penetrate through it and appear on the
      other side Singing like
      His Subjectivity.

"TILL THEN I SALUTE YOU WITH A SIGNIFICANT LOOK THAT YOU DO NOT FORGET ME"
—WALT WHITMAN

Baffling and making myself calm beyond calms or balmy as breezes
      and warm summers can be,
saying fine things, celebrating all things, hill, breast, trees,
      song, bread, body, whatever
I pass when I am fully enlightened, it awakens me,
      I awaken it, I
give the Sun the cue, I give any actor the clue,
      you make the sea and honeymoon human,
we proclaim our exchange, our intercourse, the liquid,
      ebb, tide, triumph, the motion
of all rivers, the smallest streams are sacred, the secret
      word within every waiting thing
once it is saluted makes one body and then another body and
      then another body and then another body
      on to the millennium and hum
      radiant.

MAINE VASTLY COVERED WITH MUCH SNOW

4 squirrels
are as busy as monks
looking for seeds; inside the seeds is a
      scripture;
nourishing themselves they trace their pre-history
      and future;
is theology something like the flourish of their tails ?
      alert, aware of changing seasons,

aware of other blokes about
they persist in their
scrutiny of syllables.

THE LOOK AND BOOK OF TRUTH
CAN NEVER BE UNFAITHFUL

Now it's not the 1st time that
                I see angels
                I mean snowflakes
                or that I hear music
                born out of what seems
                silence but it is the
                most necessary (is that
                easy ?) fact in the
                fabulous world of
                changing events that
                renewal is the law
                of Providence,
it occurs in strange and at times difficult and painful
                ways, death, loss of
                faith; but as I see
                all these minute
                snowflakes in the grey
                Maine day which I
cannot count any more than St. Thomas could the
                angels on a pin's head
I am consciousness of a quiet newness that I
                declare a cool and refreshing
                in some ways undecipherable
                new testament.

UNDER THE COMMANDMENTS AND
COMMOTION OF THE SUN

When I think of my letters in Post Offices or in mail bags
        before midnight or just before dawn,
on planes, in unknown corners of the universe, hundreds of

them, late at night, still or
in motion, in these hands and then those hands, in darkness
       or under fluorescent lights,
all of the letters which have a godhead in them, a spermatic
       action, processions of buffaloes,
references to angels or tomatoes, you begin to get a notion of
       how animated we are, we who are amorous
as all get out, as prolific as galaxies or herds on the
       plains of Africa. Stupendous
sumptuous insistent, productive, fertile, frequent,
       fly by night, or hidden in the shadow
of a college student at a Scottish railroad station,
       or dusted off in Andalucia,
world wide, particular, unique, impudent, asserting desires,
       desiring your ears as bees desire
       fields of flowers.

SEA PORT, THEOLOGY PORT, AIR FIELD, CELIA'S SONG, FIREFLY'S CONQUEST

I don't know where I want to go
but I want to go somewhere, I don't even know
if I want to go by plane or boat or walking or
    running
but the urge to write is there telling me that the
    sun has a message
that a child will be born, that teachers of all kinds
    will be more or less on the scene,
and activities related to instincts, like the making of birds'
    nests or the coronation of a Pope
or the singing of a girl free by the sea, the sea itself responding
    to Grand Motions,
someone is waiting to hear the symphony arranged with you
    in mind, being the Composer's
mind-reader, palm-reader, you realize every step you take,
    every boat you ride on, every ocean
    you fly over like Lindbergh or lucky
bird; later on historians at their most awake and dreamiest will
    have colorful maps of poets, ecstatic theories
    of the journey's importance.

DANCERS EMERGE FROM SILENCE LIKE FIREWORKS AND RETURN TO IT LIKE FLOWERS TO THE DIVINE GROUND

Now I have a universal audience, I am with it, the Pope himself
    tries to push near,
perhaps when I saw him with his small red cap ride by standing in
    a car and the huge crowds of the
    Roman streets were noisy
and he was going towards some token of appreciation of the
    Immaculate Conception, it was that Day,
He was respecting Silence, Silent Night, from which the Nativity
    came; I'm *not* an Orthodox Propagandist!
I was reading Thoreau who wrote "Silence is audible to all men,
    at all times, and in all places."

A WOBBLY SORT OF SAINT (SIMONE WEIL) SAID "ALL ABSOLUTE ATTENTION IS PRAYER."

Adjusting our thoughts and machinery to return to the
    wobbly world
requires need and luck; the prayers of the prayers of
        the lovers are calling the
        astronauts back to see the
        Spring day, the first yellow violet,
crocus, asphodel, daisy, weeds stirred by the wind,
        tiny fish in clear water, calling the
        acrobats of outer space back to
        hear the heart, it is beating like
        all the beginning of fish or plants or
        planets or words for you, calling the
students to become activists O wild activists of the
        very mildness of Buddha,
buds buds buds about to begin like the magnolia tree
        near Hathorn, like the gentlest
        thoughts of Hawthorne,
are calling to us . . . . . if we can listen . . . . . if we can listen

An image
is clear there then shimmers and falls very very
    deeply
into the large lake of the soul, penetrates in a
    long time and unseen
to a place which we can not name or know but
    which is unforgettable
and unforgetting, occasionally an angel, we hear a
    kind of sound, but he is
unseen touches that image now essential for us and
    changed and we
become imagistic activists by the misty lake
    with its nearby violets.

I NOTICED HOW WE WERE BREATHING

I inhaled   and held my breath
and while I was leaping I slept
and while I was sleeping I ascended higher
my bare feet weren't near the ground
I heard the sound you were making with your wings
I exhaled   I let a poem go   you and I
caught on to it and we ascended higher
until we wanted to return in order to
surprise each other again

WONDERS TO BE BORN

Take up your sound of soundlessness
      and trumpet it over the gods,
      they will be happy,
      they need you;
      keep your dignity, Musician,
      trumpet it over the gods;
      the winds are sitting by Ischia

asking about you.
The silence of a flower
writes all books.
The temple or castle or poem
in the air in the mist in the distance
is sustained by the sound of soundlessness.

O LOVELY EARTH

Going
to
sleep
while
coming
down
in
a
parachute
it
took
millions
of
years
and
now
and
then
all
around
me
were
songs
worlds
until
I
came
to
my
Self

The Greek Travel Journals
(1964-1979)

If an islander
not far from Syros,
not far from Paros,
not far from Ios,
wakes in a white town that is like purest music
by the most beautiful sea
by the most beautiful sky
surrounded by coolness and the fragrance
of flowers
if he then proceeds to walk in this
coolest and purest music
past red flowers and pink flowers and yellow flowers
and near the delicate leaves of vines
and by the sacred pomegranate tree
if he walks up and down in this
dawn, a small grey cloud
is still sleeping by a nearby mountain top,
on stone steps the edges sometimes painted white,
if he hears goat bells as he walks
up and away from the sea in order
then to slowly approach the sea,
if on some heights he sees small white domes,
a few, brightest in the cool morning light,
if I write a note home saying
"in a way
waking up in this
mountain town
is like waking up in a Persian print"
I want you to
to know that the name of this
sacred village
is Apollonia.

ARCHILOCHOS: ". . . KEEP SOME MEASURE
IN YOUR JOY—OR IN YOUR SADNESS DURING /
CRISIS THAT YOU MAY UNDERSTAND MAN'S UP
AND DOWN LIFE."

O yes   O yes
we've lived long enough to know how true that is,
    up and down, up and down,
many deep depressions, (but then again those
    curves like a woman's breasts!
The good life returns to us in perfect weather or
    perfect pleasure
    nipples showing.

GIVING VOICE AND STORY
TO ALL OUR RELATIVES

Apollo offered this
visitor a mask
and he became a brilliant actor.
Dionysus offered this
visitor a mask
and he became a dark dancer,
the community of mystified and inspired dreamers
gave the gods their names
and soon carrying olive branches the
visitors and gods
appeared on stage
enchanted, enacting
all our dreams.

"AND HERMES TOOK THE WAND WITH WHICH
HE CAN LULL TO SLEEP OR WAKE FROM THE
DEEPEST SLUMBER WHOMEVER HE WISHES."
THE ODYSSEY

Quickly
the hermetic poet took his pen
and asking it to speak its dreams
that entered the gates of that city
reminded the people of the gods; and
as goats entered the city the dreams
reminded them to be present when man
begins to lose his close touch with the earth;
the sure footed bearded ones, poets and Hermes,
affected the town by the sea so much
that Athena marvelled seeing this and
Phaecians elaborated courtesy and civilization there.

INO: "HERE THEN, TAKE THIS VEIL AND
TIE IT AROUND YOUR WAIST. WITH ITS
IMMORTAL PROTECTION YOU WILL SUFFER
NO INJURY OR DEATH." *THE ODYSSEY*

This veil
almost as transparent as the day
this artifice close to artlessness
this fabric close to fable, this light song
close to naturalness;
under a wave, under ten thousand,
Odysseus hit out
swimming, but
blessed by migrations of dolphins and
myths and songs
and the desire of Athena and Ino and
of Penelope
not confusion arrived, but the city of Phaecians
not death or injury, but Nausicaa.
Noble Odysseus awoke, sat up . . .
"Is it nymphs I hear?" he asked.

"AND THROUGHOUT THE FLEET THE HORRIBLE SCREAMS . . ." *THE ODYSSEY*

The Laestrygonian Incident
was not the last one we would have to report to
the United Nations Police Force
but it was monstrous; it seemed that hideous mountains
        ran, hairy and hungry,
they grabbed some of Odysseus' men and broke their bones,
        chewed up their meat,
speared some through the navel, made it ferociously
        impossible for a few others to reach home,
the wife of one Gigantic and Gory Laestrygonian
        gobbled one as if he were left over turkey,
another great breasted gal pressed the head
        of one long haired Achaean between
        the mountains of her breasts, each one
        weighing two tons; the clown of this
        uncivilized people spit at the sailors
        so that they felt suddenly inundated
        by the Black Sea; but some escaped;
Odysseus escaped;
and I have it on good report you escaped.

"HE IS CARRYING FROM TROY MUCH SPLENDID TREASURES, WHILE WE COME HOME EMPTY-HANDED . . . BUT COME, LET'S TAKE A QUICK LOOK AND SEE / JUST HOW MUCH GOLD AND SILVER IS IN THAT BAG." *THE ODYSSEY*

The envious
crew was torn right out of their spite and envy,
their bones flew to different parts of the earth or
        to regions so desolate they might be
        called nowhere,
their envious voices grew dimmer and dimmer
        as their envious bodies
        were part of chaos; but
during this very great time
        by sage and thyme
        by violets and sweet song

194

the acrobats of Alcinous were leaping in the delicate air
      and before landing catching a golden ball
and at this time a poet closing his eyes saw
      the Sun Recite
and at this time Nausicaa praising her maidens
      and playing by the sea
      in song with them
was preparing for the civilization of your reading;
      with envy no poem can be read,
      no journey made that amounts to discovery,
      no plan for a building that amounts to love.

ODYSSEUS: "WHO HAS MOVED / MY BED ? . . . FOR I ALONE / BUILT IT . . . / A LONG-LEAFED OLIVE TREE GREW IN THE COURT, / A FINE AND FLOUR-ISHING TREE AS THICK AS A PILLAR, / AND I BUILT UP MY BRIDAL CHAMBER AROUND IT."

What would
you want to do, displace the universe ? my bed is
      necessary, our bed is magnificent,
it's not advertisable; but I recognize it, you
      recognize it; it recognizes It;
after the mysteries were performed by us as destined
      young lovers, our life never
      forgets those early songs (nurtured
      too by the oldest nature taken so easily
      by the beginner); beginners we are
      winners, but that Tree, that flourishing
      of metaphors, those medals of music that
      our darkness made as we touched; that flourishing
      with its thickness the size of all prophecies;
what is unique about marriage
what is swift and sweet and essential about Song
          can not be moved;
look our nakedness
      imitates fish, rivers, evenings,
      seasons, gods in allegories with flowers,
look the long leafed olive tree

is making us smile as we climb
once more to the invisible
by touching all that is Sacred.

"AS DAWN AROSE FROM BESIDE HER LORD . . ."
THE ODYSSEY

Smiling
(remembering something from that night by the sea
when she saw the beauty of some birds that morning
        they reminded her of a visitor kissing her)
Dawn slowly awoke, then she put her head by his
        arm again and smiled again,
slowly she moved her leg and the shadows by the
        mountains pleased her
and looking at the small forest on his chest she smiled
        again and almost changed
the course of history by not waking up; but slowly
        she awoke
and as her light thoughts began to make musicians
        and heralds
of cocks and donkeys and goats the sea and the light
        and Athens
whispered to her lord to awake to see her in her veils
        as she walked
        across the earth
        bringing sweetness and wisdom
        to the admirers. The enlightened
        mountains and bay granted the
        holiday as usual. Dawn finding
        it natural to bring light to
        gods and mortal men also
        asked poets to sing clearly
        and readers to read with
        lightness and Hermes with
        his bright wand helped.
        And as she saw her lord
        in the distance admiring
        her procedure and knowing
        the future bliss they
        smiled again.

Look
in this mist
surrounding your home made by Athena
in this music and sleep made by the muses and Rilke and
   green ink
you begin to have an inkling of home and the clear wife and
   Ithaca to be seen,
count your treasures, take account of your poems, where shall
   we hide them
but in the radiance by our hand or sleep ? Look, Athena
   with her shining feet
walks on the beach to ask you to invent, release your
   desires;
and see how clear the mountain is becoming, how soft
   and joyous the delicate sea;
clearly Penelope waking, having dreamt of a lyre and
   a hero sleeping in a leafy tree,
is recognizing the dawn.

HELLENISTIC DERVENI BECOMES
CONTEMPORARY DERVISH

The thrashing of the dance continues
continued breaking waves the beauty
of young galloping horses the wind the
form the wind takes as it slows down
changes rises up leads the dancers the
wind dance continues the phallic play before
and during and after this raises the pitch
of hope and noise of whirling children poets
in the womb dreaming suns in the seeds
enlightening our mythologies. Ariadne carried
carried away by Dionysus, the motion of the sea
beckoning me, the foam and dancing and thrashing
of the love making continues

ARGUS VISITED SIFNOS ?

A dog
descendent of Odysseus' faithful mutt
wagging his tail often, not very good looking
but charming as it is possible
for a dog to be, jumping,
rolling over, wagging his tail,
I've never seen a friendlier mutt,
perfectly at home playing by the
sea of Odysseus, not expecting
much recognition, jumping
again, adds joy to the story.

CAPTAIN VENEZIANO

It's not shaking out the mop, he is ?
No, no, that thing there that he keeps tossing back and forth
    so that it touches the wet stone
    by the slightly tossing sea from which it came
    is magical, is marvellous, is strange,
    is mysterious, may even still be alive,
    it wouldn't be exactly right to call it
        a most marvellous witch—
        it, the source of some of my
        squirting (because of its ink)—

it's an octopus!!!

        also because
        after it gets tossed about that way
        its many soft legs fatly superbly

        hanging, dear creature of an hour,
        wet mystic described by Minoan pottery,
        one of the great wonders of the world,
        parts of it are bulging like some sort of
            prehistoric sea dirigible,

certainly it is *strange*
        and in its way

                        astoundingly beautiful

after it gets sufficiently
                moved around on land
                and in the frying pan

I probably
                in a few hours
                (Helios is now going down by
                the sea missing one of its occupants !
                one philosopher and writer who wobbled there so knowingly)

I scribbling cannibal
                orange with the sunset right now
                and though praising it-and-sunset-and-sea
                will probably enjoy eating it.

It's not shaking out the map, he is ?

THE SURVIVAL OF THE PASSING OF TIME

                "Octopus,
                octopus,
                are you listening ?
                what have I ever done for you that makes you
                        so generous for me
                supplying me with ink   year after year   century
                        after century ?"

                "What's that supposed to be, mysticism or
                        consolation of philosophy, that
                        you're squirting at me ?"

                "I call attention to you, you call attention to me and
                        the reader; Charles Darwin calls it
                        the survival of the fittest;
                        he thanks us for calling
                        attention to him—and—
                        Nature."

                "Naturally you're all wet" I heard the octopus say to the
                        new born phrase;

"listen, tough guy, who do you think you're talking to ?
if you're fit to read this you're
fit to Survive."

A ONE-MAN SHOW OF SPEED AND DEXTERITY, FIRST HE WHISTLES, THEN HE CLIMBS AND GIVES AN ARCHAIC SMILE, THEN HE LOADS THE INVISIBLE BAGGAGE AMIDST LEAVES ON THE TOPS OF THE BUSES

Hermes with his
         hat
         bright fellow
         got on top of a green bus
         and then a blue bus
         and took care of everything
         sold the tickets, dusted it off, turned on the radio,
                        got going.
Then as a bona fide
         bonus
         he put hermetical notes in every suitcase,
                        in every hand bag.
Hermes
         brightened green leaves like feathers getting taller and
         taller
         came out of his head as he was flying along up there,
         not alone,
         and his feet
         became
         you know
         lighter and Undescribable.
         CORINTH. OLYMPIA next.

By the way
         Hermes was at times green, at times blue, at times dimly
         golden.
                        He whistled again.

AN OLYMPIAN PRECEDENT

There are many ways of being witty and to woo:
                              To Wit To Woo
                              said the Owl
                              Disguised as a
                              Fable or Foolish
                              Philosopher in a
                              Tree. With
                              such width
                              and feathery
                              presence he's
                              bound to be
                              like bound
                              volumes of
                              wooing, and
                              poetic lovers
                              very close,
                              a winning
                              Representative
                              of the One.
There are many ways of watching many seasons and many songs
                              admire Athena.

GOATS, SHEEP, MAGI,
AMIDST SPECTACULAR SCENERY

          What is it the
          white goat is dreaming of
          as he chews slowly the grass
          under the orange tree in the
          mist in the rain in the sun in
          the darkness in the atmosphere
          close to the monasteries of Mistra?
          ask those old saints, they will
          tell you best of all. You in
          the bus trailing clouds of glory
          ascend and descend towards
          them in the scenery of fig trees
          thousands of olive trees and
          thousands of orange trees rich

with dark green and bright oranges,
and the magic of the travelling mist.
Ask the Magi as you approach
12th Night, Epiphany, which is
tomorrow about the oranges and about
the dream of the cluster of sheep
underneath the distant olive trees

as it drizzles for us and the churches
and the fruit high here in Mistra.

THEY GIVE EACH OTHER LAUREL BRANCHES

The gods are becoming nameless,
good, I'm glad, like cousins who disappear in the country,
like cousins who go into the forest not far away and disappear
      for a while,
when they return, you having called them, they remembering
      your drowsiness and music,
you will find them a little changed; my son went to school
      and when he returned he was a new sun;
they have to leave now and then the way a seed leaves a flower or
      the way nectar is taken from a flower
or the way dazzlement is taken from the hour; we cry; we
      look and behold
they are coming out of the forest, now find them again, sing
      of their namelessness
      as you give them
      lovely new names.
The audience of these champions is so bright that the country cousins
      still covered with dew
ask the dizzy one, the one who wants to make some spiritual
      dictionary, "are you—are you—are you
      a man or a god ?"
"Just call me country cousin" said the leafy yokel.

The French Travel Journals
(1952-1997)

THE MUSE NEAR ANTOINE

Hiding by a small Watteau he played a flute and
        she listened
while this was happening all the birds were hoping
        things would turn out well
you know how it is if one word wants the
        world to begin things
get going it amounts to wind and music in the
        mountains. When work is
a part of recreation you have eventfully
        heard the music

ART LESSON

How much time does it take you to come
how much time does it take you to be able to
        read a poem
or paint your eternal house ? if a musician
        reads a newspaper
the events become Mozart; the horse galloping
        from Grenoble park to
Grenoble park becomes more noble; grab her
        by the tail,
whisper to her Mozart Mozart, remind her
        of all the erotic paintings
        in the world.

AFTER SEEING BONNARD, MATISSE, SISLEY, MONET, WATTEAU, LORRAIN, ETC.

After spending the afternoon
with these paintings and the nearby mountains
and in the Grenoble parks and walking with Grace
        on the boulevards with many trees,
I fall asleep on a green chair; you and I in this way

listen to much unpublished music
by Debussy.

BACK IN THE TUILERIES

Birds
what were your very long time ago ancestors
        chirping about ?
the many songs that I hear you singing now in the
        Tuileries are as beautiful as can be
and your ancestors were no less geniuses, Genesis,
        and genuine;
keeping or peeping your originality is the progress that
        pleases me;
since Adam and Eve conversed with the glory of God and
        since Monet and his garden at Giverney
exchanged ideas in a similar colorful way I know
        what relative absolute success means;
        as familiar as the Word.

NYMPHEAS

AND MOMENTOUS CELEBRATION IN EVOLUTION

The green fire of green grass, Whitman salutes you,
        the green flames of his poems
        join you and
Monet Of Course; the Sun's education is
        temporal and ever vibrant;
all luminous you re-approach the way a green singer does.

Leaves are there and in the high corner of the large picture of life a
somewhat purple and green boat. Monet has not put
        anyone in the boat because
he and I were sure you, Reader, would find it
        perfect just for you.

PARTAKE WITH ALL YOUR LIGHTNESS

It is not the beard of Monet,
but the very body of his glory, accumulated
     leaves of grass,
accumulated centuries of earth and time, light
     enough for the
pitchfork of a farmer; where haloes are made;
     silence and a silo;
sickles and cycles and motions of moons; the curve
     of the earth; buttock and
breast; bees; buzzing on countless summer fields.
     Let us see It
at various hours of the Day, Light, from which more than
     the Trinity is born.
Let us join, commune, commence. We speak of the haystacks
     of Monet, accumulated Glory.

AUTOBIOGRAPHIES BLOSSOM OR
RENOIR PAINTS MONET WORKING
IN HIS GARDEN IN ARGENTEUIL 1873

It will slightly control me as I try to control it,
     it surprises us,
the wet top of my brush as I glance at bushes and blossoms
     behind a fence,
as I imagine a lingerer or listener in my dream, colors
     in vibration,
as I receive, look, as I make, wet dab of paint by
     wet dab of surprise,
words occur within the leaves; the closed or open shutters of
     the nearby house please
as your eyes do closing or opening as you smile, as you
     desire. My stance is as steady
as one excited can be as I again wet the tip of the somewhat
     magic brush. You say
hush, continue painting, hold the rainbow in your arm, near
     your heart; results will be
     a garden and a painting.

THE WINGS FAN THE FIRES

I sway,
I kneel anyway, the ship is going down, going round,
look the bed is extended, is moving, the baton or the paintbrush
        or the magician's need
consumes our molecules; the floor is the door; the sky is the
        wall; the straw chairs
the stairs the stars the fires; Arles, are you still on
        fire ? Van Gogh was at the
green window; you heard angels wrestling.

THE MUSEUMS ARE CLOSING THEIR WINGS

I close my eyes
and Van Gogh takes his much needed rest,
        turbulent pictures and all
under my eyelids; what starry nights, what
        earthquake rooms,
what fields of fire, what sunflowers, what phoenix,
        what brush strokes
have now found their temporary repose, what meteors
        have come to wait
        for a new life ?

BONNARD AND RAINBOWS
ASSISTING PROVIDENCE

A jar of honey
glowing on the breakfast table

                        a woman nearby waking up

tangerines on the table
and sunlight

                        nearby memories of Debussy
                        Monet and Impressionism

208

the smell of coffee
the sound of light

                    the sound of a woman
                    drying herself after
                    a leisurely bath

vagueness
colors   then more radiance
and warmth

the sun told the bees
the bees told the honey

the mild woman in her
soft robe of colors
appeared

                    the gentleman with the beard
                    was pleased

SOUND ADVICE TO THE SELF

I wanted to make a musical instrument
I looked at a pear
I wanted to make a musical score
I looked at a pair of lovers

I wanted to make many kinds of music
I thought of many countries, saints, lovers, fruit, flowers, etc.

I wanted to be music
so I love you

MONET SNORING

The discursive sun seeping into the sun flower
images like angels descending to sleeping people
rivers like prophets noticing slow moving clouds
raindrops like assistants joining the music of rivers

MOTHER SEWING

Seated woman
somewhat in the shade
        sewing,
light on her work, as her
        head, thoughts,
are in shadows, in the very distant
        past, childhood,
farms, need for calm designs,
        worries concerning
children on the distant seas.
        Seize the time
calmly to design a dress, embroider
        a rose. All
is passing; light, dark; all will be
        finished.

1881-82 LANDSCAPE WITH HOUSE
IN THE DISTANCE

Little quiet white house of the
        Ile de France;
bemused before this landscape, green
        field, weeds;
it might rain soon; the house like a
        white card in
the hand of fate; why do I cry? We know
        that world and lives
will turn to ghost. The host brings the fruit
        to the table that
        will disappear.

SEURAT AND HIS SUBJECTS YEAR AFTER
YEAR KNEW EACH OTHER VERY WELL

Horsecart
and solitary rider
seen from the back and
somewhat in the dark, my mother's
        father

often left at 4 in the morning from one
          little town
to another little town to buy grain; he
          and the
horses and the grain knew each other very well.

THE ALWAYS EARLY WORK OF THIS LOVER;
THERE'S A POINTILLISM TO IT

Being a speck in a spectacle,
being a light amidst many moving lights, galaxies,
          a farmer to be in a world
          to be my ever changing lover,
I hoe, I praise Seurat, I plant seeds, I
          touch lettuce,
I know dew and you, the shelter of the shade is
          colorful, as
delicate as a rainbow, as precise and determined
          as Seurat,
he praises us being picturesque about it. Sundays
          are sacred, every moment is a holiday,
          when he has made his touch.
          Sleep is colorful too.

INSTRUMENTALIST OF SOME
SEASONS AND REASONS

Slender
as a thin branch in winter
as a slightly curved wet branch in spring
          the mysterious
Musician (melancholy ? hunger artist ?) with
          his trombone
performs; forms of hats, of anonymous shadow
          like creatures
in Plato's world, come and go. Step by step,
          day by day,
give us this day our daily breath, speck by
          speck, respecting
reality we are shadows; the mist rises, the
          notes of the
odd trombonist or dilapidated prophet flicker
          like leaves
          in fall.

211

FERVENT STRONG MUSEUM
GUARD AS QUIXOTE

Dreams of glory:
to be a museum guard ardent
    quixotic
cooperative in *all* the museums of
    the world,
to project the Images, to welcome the
    children
and the contemplatives from every
    walk of life,
to collect within myself and transform
    all this
into some continuing undercurrent
    that surfaces
now and then which manifests
    in all directions some
    sort of love.

QUIETNESS; "THE ARTIST'S
MOTHER EMBROIDERING"

Stitch by stitch,
point by point, delicate
    concentration,
care, design by design; modest,
    fine, no
safeguard for the genuine and the soul
    stronger than
    modesty.

SEURAT; SUNSET; OR ARRIVAL

House at Dusk; who is
    waking up,
who is going to sleep ? who
    senses the
infinite loneliness and quietly belongs
    to his ancestors,
assents to his fate, chooses the
    right crayon or
paint brush, when necessary,
    chooses prayer.

"The Mower," 1881, "recalls
    Millet's work,"
recalls Van Gogh, recalls all
    the work, all
the wheat in the fields. We bow to
    bring food, we work
to continue life.

"THE HIGH COLLAR; LADY IN BLACK"
"THE VEIL" "THE ARTIST'S MOTHER"

Only known slightly,
all, everything, if "known" at all,
    shadows,
figures with fine deportment, unique,
    seen sometimes
in a soft halo of light; what images are
    seen in a church?
flickering of candlelights; singular figures,
    sometimes seen
from the back, or in profile; gently
    imagined in
all their privacy, temporary attitude, integrity,
    point by point
assumed in the procession; something is necessarily
    veiled if it is
vital; something point by point, delicate absolute
    attention, revealed,
respected. No invasion of privacy, nothing advertised.
    A few quiet gestures,
words, restraint, in the darkness of the room.
    The artist's mother
as if seen dimly in candlelight; no fluorescence,
    no commerce;
one aware of destiny, of fate, these specks of light
    in soft darkness, these
    flickerings of worlds.

"AT PONTAUBERT"

In the forest
what raindrops have fallen

this misty morning ? the trees grow, the
      trees die;
one by one my ancestors die; my mother;
      and I;
do you see this ? look there look there
      it stirs . . .

"THE CLEARING; LANDSCAPE WITH A STAKE"

I want to leave a mark
      so
I won't be altogether lost; some
      brother
might a century from now come and
      find
the little harp; or this sketch; I have
      a secret
signal for you perhaps; who is waiting
      for me
after these days of rain? beauty is a signal too
      designedly dropped.

TROUBLED TEMPORARY SKY,
TROUBLED TEMPORARY RIVER

Steamboat
in the dark dark
on some river anywhere anywhere
      where
are you taking those familiar strangers who
      chanced
into this world, do I see my sister
      weeping there like
      some lost angel?

RAPPORT, ROUTINE, IN ESSENTIAL MYSTERY

Standing bent-over gardener in his
      white shirt
somewhat glowing like the unseen sun
      eventually
to come; mysterious often responding earth,
      dark world.

ACCEPTANCE AND PERSISTENCE

Stone Breaker
before the sun rises
making his daily difficult effort
        in much darkness
alone in the fields; unseen face;
        white shirt; anonymous
worker in his silence in repeated
        darkness.

"FARM WOMEN AT WORK" (1882-83)

Two bulky delicate farm workers
        bending over
in the fertile field at work; an expert
        centuries-educated
familiar touch is knowlegeable, precise.
        Assisting growth,
assisting children, people, in need of
        food, wisdom,
ritual, these women serve as strength, models in
        our hope.

THE DREAMER DRAWS THE DREAMER

I'm drawn to it, haunted quietly
        in a way,
to this subject "Gateway" "View
        from a
Balcony" "Place de la Concorde,
        Winter";
light, dark; a tree; a silhouetted
        figure; drawn;
it is, I am, you are, significant.

PASTIME

Monkey in profile with distended tail;
Woman with bustle, tall, elegant, fishing;
you've got to do something once the molecules
        have put you here.

ALL ABSOLUTE AFFECTION
IS SACRAMENTAL

Woman
with pretty little hat and
        in profile
and with narrow waist and
        curve of a
bosom; conté crayon conceived;
        welcomed by
Seurat as a subject; he and we are objects of designs'
        Affection.

SUNDAY, SPECKS, AND
COLORS IN THE PARK

The Couple
woman with umbrella and
        petit bustle
strolling with her somewhat
        obliterated perhaps
bored gentleman in his Sunday
        top hat in the
Park. Trying to be as "dignified" and
        elegant as
possible, they are as perfect subjects
        as monkeys
once the wit of Seurat sees them and
        his colors create
        them and us.

BIRD MARKS ON THE SAND;
BODY LANGUAGE IN THE WIND

In the Circus
one does one's stunt,
leap high upside down,
feet flapping in the air,
body like a ribbon that
can blow away in the wind,
entertaining for others who are
passing, temporary scherzo,
individual, colorful, all
bemused and coming to death.

YOUR VOICE IS SOMEWHAT CHANGED
BUT YOU SLIGHTLY RECOGNIZE YOURSELF

A man makes a sketch,
a boy with a black cap makes
      an echo,
you sometimes echo me the life said
      to the poem;
increasingly so; you are amused by the
      turn of the
planets, the messages from plants; the
      Seurat pastime.

IN PROFILE, AND IN A SOMEWHAT
LOOSE DIM BLUE DRESS

A woman seated on the grass
      is more
than a monument, more than a
      pyramid,
her shadow tells time, her
      embroidery
makes rhyme. A little at a time
      one shows
one's respect, one makes one's
      collection of
poems. I am trying to listen to her
      all the time.

SOMEWHERE BETWEEN ST. DENIS
AND PARIS I THANK YOU

Field of Alfalfa near
      St. Denis
from A to Z you've been
      teaching
me how each separate short brushstroke
      or blade of
grass instructs instructs; as we become
      introspection
we look on the instructive world.

Rhythm
of shapes of hats, rhythm of
     shapes
of bodies, rhythm of gradations
     of changing
colors, rhythm in other words
     attracts
entertains an audience, makes
     meanings,
whatever; the one night stand of
     musicians
or mimes on the bandstand,
     saltimbanques
and others appear, disappear; the
     lights of the
showplace suggest stars, look
     like flowers;
for a few hours we listen to the
     delicate French
     trombonist.

THREE LIVES

PARIS	CÉZANNE	YOUR NAME
Apples	by	painting
oranges	step	order
music	park	by
mathematics	by	love
Paris	park	clarity
Cézanne	painting	by
step	by	ecstasy

NON-POSSESSIVE LOVE

When an onion becomes a saint
when a bottle becomes a saint
when an object becomes a subject
when an object becomes a soul
when a soul is clear and cool and colorful
and imagined and constructed you are
     still alive with Cézanne.

THE BEAUTIFUL VACATION OF
RENOIR'S *A LA GRENOUILLERE*

If you're sitting out at a good very good
     country restaurant
and the country is as mild and very very warm and as
     idyllic as France and heaven can be
and if you are a Renoir fulfilled calm woman
     as satisfied and peacefully
     delicate and alive as can be
and you see some of this truth as if reflected in
     a glass of cool water
you can forever drink at the fountain of youth;
     soul; song; light.

IN THE VAST PALAIS DE TOKYO IN PARIS

Who knows what this little gnat is doing in the
     Post-Impressionist Museum,
prehistoric and post-impressionist,
relative to Seurat and Mozart and the
     surprising moment.

CONCERNING SOME SAINTS
AND IMPRESSIONIST PAINTERS

halo.

And
when
they
left
it
is
only
just
and
poetic
and
practical
that
they
left
only
their

IN ADDITION IN THE DISTANCE THE EIFFEL
TOWER IMITATES A FLOWERY PROPAGANDIST

Why do your arms keep imitating birds
        may I ask you
        may I
        well May arrived
and I didn't ask again until next year but
        I was sky writing
        like a bee
I was making a fortune to give away to my cousins by flying over
        France with
        the paintings of Matisse
        and Chagall tied to my
thought; you think so ? it looks as if their paintings are kites
        and you readers
        are kicking your
        feet in joy as you

hold on to them and me
flying over Paris and its dreams

CÉZANNE SAID: "FLOWERS I HAVE GIVEN UP. THEY FADE IMMEDIATELY. FRUITS ARE MORE FAITHFUL. THEY LIKE TO HAVE THEIR PORTRAITS PAINTED."

Cézanne, say what you want, but I feel flowers
        are faithful also,
and so is a tree, faithful to its own flowering or
        leafy flourishing, as
fruits are faithful to their fruitfulness, and
        poems to the
poet, so is death that Whitman sang to, flourishing,
        appropriate
to nature; it's a matter of time; flowing vibrations
        of colors, of desires,
it's a matter of streams, I consider them faithful too;
        we are such
things as streams are made of and our lives surrounded
        by faithful sleep.

NEEDED, AMIDST THE CONTRASTS

What is going to make us
        feel cool ?
a scene of Bathers by Cézanne or a
        melody by
John Coltrane ? good to have a green thought in a
        green shade;
amidst all the molecular action that is
        going on in me
and eruptions and rhythms in nature out there and
        everywhere, some
coherence and coolness, a few blue tones by Cézanne,
        help establish

what seems like strength and sanity; needed amidst
    the contrasts.

YEATS: "THINGS FALL APART . . ."; AND THE COMPOSER OF CUBES, CALM COLORS, TONE POEMS

Did you feel the world was about
    to die
that you constructed it so carefully ?
    here, sacred
tone, here, sacred apple, flower, table,
    card player;
did you, Uncle Cézanne, feel an earthquake
    was about
to happen ? that you built up our strength,
    that you
    Composed.

CÉZANNE'S ROOM

How did he look at a glass so as to
    make it
a canto of Paradise, something clear,
    a sacrament,
a thing not asking for anything? the purity
    of that
struck us dumb as if we saw the Lord on the
    road to
Damascus; now you are soaring; we might ask
    of it
to be a symbol, an object divined by Cézanne;
    we will
do it no harm by drinking the water whatever our
    mood or
interpretation; but to see with the eyes of Cézanne !
    to visualize,

make palpable, make part of his purest communication
     with me,
this substance this light of water, that baffles
     the sages.
From within my admiration of his vision, his art,
     I too
for a moment become pure.

FOUNTAINS AND STATUES AND AMAZED TOURISTS BETWEEN NOTRE DAME AND THE ORANGERIE

To have
had the heart or admiration or joy lifted
     the way
Apollinaire lifted a poem, the way our gaze lifts
     the Eiffel Tower;
the way Paris clearer in sunlight and springtime than
     ever before lifts us;
from Pont Neuf you take off, in the Tuileries you see
     Marcel Marceau
with a single flower or Monet with a thousand canvases.
     Pavlova, how
can you get on your toe that way ? What are you doing
     spinning and spinning
and spinning out in the universe and so
     close to my heart ?

Beginning of Acknowledgment

Reading aloud with friends
>allowing for differences
>of intonations and destinies
>we give each other the Dickens
>or proceed with Propertius, wager
>that Virgil will remain vital, follow
>him with Dante and then ascend with Beatrice,
>go all the way to the end of the novel or poem
>until we are in the empyrean of memory; we
remember our differences and affections together, each taking what
>he or she can, each in a slightly different region
>of a canto or connotation of a phrase finding
>identity and community.

SONNET 18: "SO LONG AS MEN CAN BREATHE OR EYES CAN SEE, / SO LONG LIVES THIS, AND THIS GIVES LIFE TO THEE."

We don't know exactly
>what's going to happen
>when we take up the pen
>when we touch the woman
>when we look at the flowering magnolia
>when the sky is all saffron and golden
or this morning when I begin for the last time a Writing Course,
>I encourage them, who are they, they often wonder too,
>that mystic synthesis brings us in to speech, gestures;
how momentary the messages are, the lives of fireflies and galaxies are,
we don't exactly know, but what is precisely called forth now
>this late April morning before the
>darling buds of May begin to
>shake is exact adventure is
>exact beginning of
>acknowledgment.

AROUSED TO EXTENSIONS

Poems are so fast, they run ahead of you,
        have nothing to do
with fashion or with trade; when you are
        hiding then slow
readers will catch up? once your poems were
        unseen ahead of you,
you finally met; it was epiphany, it was
        Event. Some
were heaven bent, you were heaven sent. It's true.
        Light grows
I know. I see it on your body, on my hands
        once I have
touched your body. We sight the universes as we die
        and then return.
Dante too in Paradise began to sense the breezes from
        the angels' wings,
songs came your way; I sense it from the way you
        look at me.
So far ahead of me the light that love taught your eyes.
        Count countless
Cantos or just begin, then wish for me, wait for me;
        I hear your voice.

WHITMAN AND I AND OTHERS AND
THE LANGUAGE EXPERIMENT

Adjectives and Adverbs—how I love you, how you help
        qualify me, the changing
weather, the mountains that rise and fall, the slow
        procedure of the snail, verbs
and nouns and prepositions for you, for me,
        pronouns and different tenses,
tension, pauses, release, explosions, exclamation marks
        and other forms of opera,
how I need and thank you, assistance to Keats and
        love letters, lyrics and
you and me. I say all festivals, Chinese, Italian,
        New Orleans, Thanksgiving,
communications and celebrations of all kinds are helped by you,

I would like to be within
you forever, to have you go out to friends and strangers, to make
        their-our grammatical construction
        democratic-theological.

MERLIN

I am the motion in the leaves
I am the music in rivers finding their greenness and rhythm
I am the flowers in stars finding their expression
I am the desire to touch you on the palms of my hands
which reads our fortunes and stirs our dreams
I am the dream that is like a winged serpent
that dances in the dark before your swaying body
that dances like a flame before your disguised tree
that prances and spouts like a comic masked actor
before your mystic body your creating sea:
the green of your darkness
and the green of my sperm.

AS I WALK ON A SUNNY DAY NEAR THE END OF JULY ON A CURVING COUNTRY ROAD, MANY GNATS AND WILDFLOWERS, WEEDS AND MUCH BREEZE

Notebook,
I carry you with me wherever I go,
        or
Notebook, you carry me with you, giving
        me a
temporary noteworthy direction, perhaps even
        caring
for me when some say I am gone. Daily diary,
        dire necessity,
as somewhat thoughtful lovers, I touch upon you,
        you reflect
my selectivity and how I sentence myself.
        Lightweight

to make our motions' life lighter.
                    I take note
of us as now I walk high in the upstate N.Y.
                    country mountains of a
                    million tiny daisies.

FOLLOWED BY THOUGHTS OF WORDSWORTH AND THE LAKE COUNTRY

I enter my Studio in the morning about the same time
                    that the sun enters
my studio or just before, very rarely after; right now
                    I see how it is making
the shadows of the few leaves remaining on the autumn tree near
                    my window flicker a little bit
on the illuminated wall in front of me above my typewriter;
                    it's quiet and private, and yet
somehow open, at the moment undisturbed like the light at the
                    surface of a calm small lake.

DISCOVERING MORE THAN AMERICA

I want to know where I am—so I write a poem.
I want to know that I am—so I write a poem.
                    Then you get involved, with
whatever I see, remember, or think I'm desiring,
                    and so we go on
proposing, procreating, praising, raising children and
                    vegetables, making
the sentences longer; clouds drift by magnificently changing
                    their shapes day after day
                    year after year.

DESIRE ME AND YOU MIGHT
RECEIVE PLENTY OF MAIL

Since I'm always looking for excuses for walking
    let me walk
towards you, writing is a form of walking, by foot,
    by measure, by
rhythm, by surprising turn of events or phrases,
    barefoot or in shoes of
different cultures, in moods of different magnificence or
    silliness I saunter,
I wish, I whistle, I wince, I win, I bring my poems
    slowly or in a hurry
in any changing season of the Moment to you, lady or reader,
    of my desire.

TRADUTTORE / TRADITTORE

no matter
how familiar
every one's a bit of a foreign language
sometimes we learn a few more words a few more
        sentences
sometimes we forget what we learned as we
        proceed as more or less
        translators / traitors

PROPHETIC NECESSITIES

Getting the phrases right
the authenticity of the phases of the moon
or the meandering of a stream; you maybe have seen
        flying over
Minnesota miles and miles below in a beauty that
        is opulent
also in opals patterns of meanderings, it is as if
        the gods free

and improvising knew that we needed designs, no
        one can define
or predict a design, but there are prophecies all
        over the place.

*

When I am feeling blank
blank as a blank piece of white paper
I take up my pen and say "Mark Me"

and Hamlet in his inky coat appears

I say Mark Twain and my stream of consciousness
begins to be at length novel

I say I always praise and thank my
humorous and saintly teacher Mark Van Doren

Now the field is no longer blank,
active reader, you have us to thank.

VOWS, VIOL, VIOLA, VOWEL, VIBRATIONS

Writing a poem often at blessed best is like Arion
        riding on the dolphin's back,
no one knows where the dolphin comes from, but
        the poem holding on to the dolphin
senses it, senses they were meant for the
sound love, for the journey or sentences rhythmically
        in need of arriving at your
        shore. Your surety, you
surely being there, reminds us of success, epiphany, the
        unbreakable music of *12th Night*.

TYPED FAREWELL SCENARIO

Some people
may feel towards their cars the way I feel towards you,
        old typewriter,
maybe the way Louis XIV felt towards his favorite horse and
        carriage, anyway
I hate to give you up, Smith Corona Galaxie Deluxe, even
        though you are
getting quite dilapidated (and what about me   ?), even though at
        times you don't
function properly; for so many years you've carried me to where
        my poems wanted to go,
for so many years I fingered you, pounded you, heard you,
        you with all your
letters of the alphabet and semi-colon and question mark., *etc.*
        and exclamation point   !
I sentimentalize like Richard II at his abdication   ?   anyway I'll
        prolong the farewell a few more
        days;   a few more months   ?

VERY MUGGY JULY DAY AND TRYING
TO WORK THINGS OUT WITH
A COMPLICATED NEW TYPEWRITER

Good morning, I said to the new electronic typewriter,
        I trying to be
as patient and practical and precise and mechanical as is
        possible for
a person more related to mist and flora and fauna than to
        mechanics and electronics;
I guess that's part of your riverlike pursuit, you want to
        personify the world
and the new typewriter and the new reader;   you're exercising
        patience as you
        perspire and
        perspire.

A SORT OF LECTURE

Dr. Wms.,
      you wrote poems on the typewriter
         when you were not delivering babies
and so
      following your example
      I get my typewriter out
         in my school office
            and write between lectures,
the lectures are babies too,
      we're not quite sure what they will say,
         how they will turn out,
we're democratic and hopeful about them,
         babies and poems and lectures;
I wonder if the professors lecturing about poetry   will be
      disturbed by the sound of
         writing of poetry ?
William Carlos Williams, more life to you, you who gave
      more life
         to poems and babies,
            the pedantic rest can be laid to
               rest quietly . . .

NOT FAR FROM THE ANDROSCOGGIN RIVER,
SEPTEMBER 17TH

Well
    what
        can I do for you
            William Carlos Williams
    that all your million and one poems
        and
           Paterson birds
              and patients
haven't
    already done
        there by St. Francis and Einstein and the
               daffodils and winds
    players
        from all over

                                    have praised you
                                        and having knocked at
                                            your door
returned   home
        with more poems
                    their own
                            and yours
it's on your birthday that I want to tell my class
        look him up
                you'll find him
                            still typing
                                    in

poetry's paradise.

WM. CARLOS WILLIAMS' "TO A DOG
INJURED IN THE STREET"

" . . . . . . René Char
                    you are a poet who believes
in the power of beauty
            to right all wrongs.
                I believe it also.
With invention and courage
        we shall surpass
                the pitiful dumb beasts,
let all men believe it,
        as you have taught me also
                to believe it"

A REQUEST RELATED TO
WILLIAM CARLOS WILLIAMS

We don't know
            what it will be like
                    the next life
or what the 5 letter abstraction, death, will be for the
        individual body,
                    the individual soul,

and like Icarus
        that disappears
                in the landscape,
can't know now what
        the past was
                so we make the supreme fictions,
seek to define ourselves
        somewhat
                as we make
patterns in the sand or
        all the portraits in the Louvre
                as we pronounce
laughingly love love, language
        how we need you
                inadequate as you are;
a foolish reason for feeling
        inadequate
                incomplete
but how can we and Ulysses and Dr. Paterson be complete
        without
                including history, the cosmos,
the cousins and what all the tribes call in different ways
        God or the
                Nameless One;
you haven't gone too far; you have come here
        to say Paterson, Lewiston, Paris,
                to become
geographer, to reconcile moment and
        object, subject, and place,
                vibrations,
I have come here to ask myself and you to eventually
        finish—or just celebrate—
                all the poems in the world.

IF FINAL EXAMS COME CAN
HEAVEN BE FAR AWAY ?

I feel as if I'm in prison and I'm only in school, it's
        a beautiful
Spring day, daffodils are livelier than
        Wordsworth, I yawn
I pace before the students taking a two-hour test

236

about the late Romances
in Shakespeare, there is a smell of sneakers,
        there is a smile of
the Mona Lisa and the free Autolycus. Outside
        there is a honk of a school bus
that is about to take some kids to play
        baseball; I am not
sixteen; I have been tested 35 years in my pacing
        and Reciting
way as I have presented daffodils, daring enactments
        of KING LEAR storms, solemn or
        daffy constant "coming to terms
        with Great Literature"!
"Bodhisattva" Allen Ginsberg called me before
        getting on the plane;
"Bodhisattva voice exercises" I reply as
        I sigh, yawn, look skyward,
        kiss a poem as it flies.
After 35 years of so-called "teaching" I am sort of like
        Romeo who wisely said:
"Love goes towards love as schoolboys from their books,
But love from love, towards school with heavy looks."

WHERE ARE ALL THE POETRY BOOKS
IN YOUR HOUSE ?

In a way very few people seem to be interested in
        poetry
and yet they wouldn't in a way have a leg to stand on if
        if weren't for poetry
just as Shiva wouldn't if it weren't for OM;
        nevertheless
people are really interested in the poetry which is
        before the words and
        after the words of
the poetry; they have their needs but it takes them a
        long time to get around
to It; poets don't suffer because of this, they just have
        a certain priestly privacy and
send their regards and hiccups and prayers to
        future audiences.

FOR THE NEW BOOK OR NEW BOOKSTORE

O you who read books O you who cooperate with poems
      looking always for some god
behind a tree or within a word you will see that
      the Shinto priests will
appear and shake their leaves, how can you forget
      the ritual of the two slow moving
      dancing priests high in the
mountains of a Japanese island as the flute music played as the
      mist was reminiscent of great
      Chinese and Japanese paintings
and as the downpour of rain was the heaviest most
      joyous downpour of rain,
and then there was Dylan "his decks are drenched with
      miracles / miracles of fishes . . ."
O you who wander on the cliffs of words on the mountains
      of metaphors by the sea and sound of
      similies, you who are
resounding in the religious cooperation, you have bookstores
      and new years and gods to support.

THE LOVER, THE READER, AND
THE CLOWN ABOVE THE CITIES

The clown's coming out of the tent,
watch out, the flower's coming out of the ground,
the sun and clouds watch the various skies,
the fireman's coming out of the fire, this time
having seen everyone; the dirigible is coming
out of the church-like locker room; he leaps
into the sky with various skies in his arms;
the astronaut is coming out of his co-operative
venture with all the flags of all nations
flapping like butterflies around his helmetted ears;
the reader is emerging from the tent of a poem
dressed like a flying clown and he follows
his balloons of all colors which he gives to all lovers.

THERE ARE MANY BRIGHT WITNESSES

The tiger
in the fire wandered here and there
that warm night and spoke into the laps of
       maidens in their huts
       surrounded by hibiscus and monkeys
       and waiting jeweled snakes
and with one paw uplifted whispered to the ears
       of prophets
to take up their brooms and dance; they brushed
       them against the stars
       once, twice, three times
and when the orange stick took fire they went
       into the huts
       surrounded by prayers
       surrounded by pools
       surrounded by weeds
       surrounded by moons giving lucky numbers
       surrounded by insects carrying on a festival
and they set the sacred house on
       fire, they touched it,
and with the ability to carry fire
       and dance two inches above the ground
they ran around shouting poems.

FOR A BLOND FELLOW WHO SAW THEM
IN AFRICA—BILL MCDIARMID

I heard of a hill of
       giraffes once
       1st still   like meditators in highest regard
       and part of God's high regard for Scenery

then
suddenly
all in motion

       there are countless other fables
       flames   leaping from the Sun
       dancers   in THE DREAM

```
        wind              thought
but this was in its own way


exact
surprising
perfect


              hundreds of giraffes
              on a hill   suddenly in motion
```

WHILE ON HER VACATION IN NOVA SCOTIA ON THE BEACH MY SISTER-IN-LORE FINDS THIS EMBLEM LONG, ELEGANT AND SUBLIME

A clue from an angel ?
better than a relic from a saint ?
part of a wing of some long winged sea bird ?
a moment of divine music or the elongated saying of the
          sea spray made long and ivory like ?
some dream artifact of an Eskimo mystic ? guess what it is,
          guess what it is if you can or
mystic mammal spouting that you are, get into the sea, the
          seas, all thoughts,
and wander wander after it, hearing its songs, its notes
          of biblical and sexual innuendoes,
its cadenzas of delicate oceans; wander wander as merman
          or mermaid as propitious urgency
after it so that you will say when you as a baby with
          a bib or a reader of natural hieroglyphics
          find the whale's tooth
you are a musical ancient indication of Leviathan, you
          are an emblem of the Wandering Temple
          in blubber and Song of the
          Lord of all Hosts.
Whistle a tune to it, to Magnificent It, as best you can—
"A tooth, a tooth ! my library for a tooth !" said
          the wise old man.

YOUR TALE IS DECORATIVE ENOUGH

Sure footed practical one, nearby
    frequent
well-balanced visitor, you seem
    to know
what to major in, how to stop and
    think so as
to entertain the observer, how to
    scamper quickly
from branch to branch, squirrel, your
    enterprise
amidst the leaves seems precise; direct
    and hungry
you get to the very kernel of knowledge.

WE SPEAK AN UNTRANSLATABLE BUT EVER PRESENT COMMON LANGUAGE

First we were fish? I knew there was something
    fishy about you;
then we were birds? I know sometimes we are
    flighty; what about
the rest, snakes, monkey business, restlessness?
    I like
animation, graceful, instinctive animals, rebirth
    of earthiness
in us and expansive sky like thoughts, dances and
    planetary motion.

RELIGIOUS RECOGNITION AND NEED

Small tree
before the entrance to my school office
what was your name? every day I admired
the shape of your generous complex thin branches
the ecstasy of that and the recurring abundance in proper time

in the prepared season of your amplitude of so many small flowers
you made a circle that Fra Angelico and his angels would have applauded
my belief is that they were involved and celebrating, were making me
see, I often have a sense of choruses of assurance when I am in
ecstasy; and so, small close relative, that in all seasons had
unique beauty and helped me teach whatever it was that day,
today seeing you cut in small pieces after your death in
the lightning recent fierce summer storm crucifixion
dismemberment shocked I mourn, I realize
mortality, I sense that unity that wants
the dream of immortality

A FEW MOMENTS AGO THEY WERE TIGHTER, MORE CLOSED

By the second they seem to be getting enlightenment,
    these bodhisattvas,
they teach me at once something undescribable but
    very visible and
beautiful about maya and nirvana, I pass their
    father and mother
magnolia tree often as I walk to get a book or
    mail a letter,
and beginning now in early May in Maine to flower,
    Preservers of
the light, dispensers of the fragrance, messengers of recurrence,
    enigmatic scripture
    giving buds.

FREEDOM AND THE FREQUENT FLYER BONUS

These above noises,
these planes flying overhead while I'm reading
    a poem,
I wonder where all those uplifted people
    strapped in
are going, they must all have some hope of some

Meeting,
some "meaningful event," something to further their being,.
            but what
a come down it often is and they find themselves with
            their mostly
perennial chemistry, problems and often prosaic situation.
            Blake transports
me perfectly to where the Lamb and Tiger were made, to
            the soul and its songs of
            Innocence and Experience.

WE MAKE GOOD TIME

Bushes and trees, ample, abundant, exorbitant,
            calm
rich and varied as can be in coolness and the
            sumptuous sun
seen and sung to me by centuries, your ancestors'
            voices chorusing
carousing as I ride by on a Bus called Bonanza
            from Providence
to New York, Whitman's New York and more, Allen Ginsberg's
            New York and more,
my sister's New York and more. Trucks and truck drivers on
            the road as companions
instead of whales; the ample air and blue sky is larger than
            leviathan; we are all
in some sort of growth, splurge, death is too, cycles of
            change more than any
of the machinists' wheels that speed us on these American
            superhighways; mile after
mile of bushes, trees, large, wide, in the giving season
            between Spring and Summer.
Pilgrims and Indians in your past, in your shadows; chipmunks
            and woodchucks and chickadees,
and birds in hiding; now and then an occasional gasoline station;
            we whizz by you all,
now I remember it's Flag Day; our varied songs wave
            the American banner
but above it the united states of the world banner,
            numerous, particular,

undefinable unique people and indefinite commentators; fine
          wide highway by
amplitude of thriving forth giving gods, bushes and trees.

SOUL IS A PORT IN AIR THAT TOOK DOMINION EVERYWHERE

Arrival ?
what do you mean by arrival ?
you might imagine a climax, that a moment
          arrives or a
cadence or wave rises; and there is of course
          Venus
arriving out of the sea or an early Apollo or
          dawn
itself, but the so seen arrival has a beginning
          God knows
where; the weather and oceans change and the
          music and
our Apollo and Venus and Dionysus like stuff
          of consciousness,
and what imaginative dreamers-lovers call the
          universe-and-God,
its arrival-and-commotion baffles me. So we wonder
          about arrival;
what we know is the need for Noah to sail towards
          God with all
his animals and alphabets; what we arrive at is
          a mortal's
mysterious Comedy which again and again and again
          arrives at
making different names for love, for all journeys
          towards you.

THE INTEGRITY OF A SCENE

Puzzles,
you temporarily puzzle me

but with our original integrity
we get our act together; so we are
      not broken up
permanently; it is a game of finding what part
      relates to what
other part; here or there we fit in, our
      colors coordinate and
jive; it's quite a job for Job at times; patience
      is much required.
Patience and play and please puzzle me together; I, we,
      have many selves; it
takes time and search, reconstruction, reformation;
      United We Stand World Wide
      or side by side rest
      colorfully in love
      Together.

PLATO: "WONDER IS THE BEGINNING OF PHILOSOPHY."

What
is a poem going to do with
      all this
snow? one could imagine making
      a snow man,
one could imagine the soft snow as a
      precipitation
of large soft clouds and now that
      children
can walk on, sleigh ride on, then one
      could go
on imagining into transcendence, Spring and
      warmth
coming and the snow fulfilling streams, the
      snow giving
help to some future flowers. If you are
      energetic and
      imaginative and wordy enough you could go on as long
      as there is
      Wonder.

To be
     king of the Rocks—
     that's better than being Philip of Macedonia
     or Alexander in India; I had only responsibilities
          to my
     Imagination and to the hard edged terrain of the boulders
          not far
     from my Father's Italian restaurant overlooking in the
          distance
     railroad tracks, cat tails, and a New Jersey swamp;
          these boulders
     were often huge, slanted, flat at the top, perfect for
          Robin Hood
     and for young boys to have their adventures; I was the
          movie director
     and we would jump from one high place to another
          in this way
     conquering Mesopotamia, Macedonia, and Secaucus.
          I was Napoleon
     or Caesar or some American cowboy, we got scratched
          in mock battle
     occasionally but never killed; once I lost my
          Mickey Mouse wrist watch,
     those theatrical rocks were on a hill and when the snow melted
          and I was months older
     the 5 and 10 cent store watch was found and it
          worked perfectly.
     There was no purpose to these leaping phases or phrases
          other than conquest
     by Play. We expended energy with incomparable abandon;
          danger and exhilaration
     prepared me for the life of art. Goats and dragons could have been
          our companions
          with ease.

THE INFINITE ENTERS THE FINITE,
THE MUSIC BECOMES PARTICULAR

Pulsating heart in my left ear,
            are you a metronome ?
            more or less steady in your
            continuity, another measure,
            another expression of I go, I come,
I enter the universe palpitating like an amoeba or the conditions
            that go with it, rhythmical
            somehow; I think of the
planets as Noh actors that slowly turn, each motion somehow
            affecting the motion of the
            other; the gestures of
seasons in slow entrances, exists; a tick, a tock, a rock,
            a beating of some need that
            made me and you sends out
suggestions for symphonies, myths that include stars and all the
            religious hopes, the hope that
            Juliet is on the balcony again.

JULIET: "THE MORE I GIVE, THE MORE I HAVE..."

It seems to me
that if some smart aleck or even an encyclopedia of
            a Harvard wizard
could tell us what "perfection" is that the definition
            would be tremendously
imperfect; the genetic nature, instinct, sensibility
            of every life in ever
changing creation must though we are all remotely and
            intimately related
must find its own way and when all our lives
            are over we can
look back upon the little earth and all its
            myriads of miracles,
of changing types of people, as Dante in heaven,
            and amazed say
It Happened; there are no maps for lovers;
            but when they

have given themselves away completely there'll be
    no need for definitions.

COLERIDGE: "WE RECEIVE BUT WHAT WE GIVE."
ROBERT FROST: "AND FORTHWITH FOUND
SALVATION IN SURRENDER."

Subjects for poetry? endless.
Start with song of myself and go on
        out from there,
start with song of any other, object or cosmos
        and go on in from there,
the process, the proceeds, will be the same.
        What gift outright
you, gifted one, can give will save the cycles
        from being soundless,
will save the moments from being meaningless.

SPIRIT APPEALS TO THE SENSES . . .
AND BE SENSIBLE IN EVERY HELPFUL WAY

Beating heart,
what are you trying to tell me in my left ear ?
that there is ticking, that time has angels in it ? one with
        his little hammer
or rhythmic breath repeats something to my perforated ear.
        What is it?
that Being has its blood stream, that Being has its notes of
        music ? soon
I believe it will be Bach's Birthday Again; he returns with
        those fugues and angels
for all ears; Reception is grander than all Baroque churches.
        Being palpitates
as lovers in Verdi do. Doing one's best to hear the sublime, the
        longevity of poetry
became longer than the longest ears of the invisible endless
        Buddha. Beating heart,
tell them, the Shakespearean lovers and the others, the Wordsworth wonders,

that we love and need
to hear them.

THE SPEECH OF EACH UNIQUE VOICE

Everything
is a message, a motion for us, in some way one of
        our thoughts,
the quick graceful silver fish in the stream, the millions
        of fish suddenly
changing their direction in the ocean, the sea anemone,
        the plant by our
window sill, the slant of light on winter afternoons, not
        making noises,
but whether we are somewhat aware of it or not, sending us
        vibrations, colors,
messages, that become part of the tone of our body, the
        gesture towards you, the
        sound of this poem.

"ALTISSIMU ONNIPOTENTE, BON SIGNORE, TU SO LE LAUDE, LA GLORIA, E L'HONORE . . ."
SAN FRANCESCO

How much attention span can you
        give a prayer
without restlessness and your so called mind
        wandering ?
can it span the world, can it span a flower ?
        spend your attention
on this leaf, this bud; that's how Buddhism
        began; learn to
hold on by letting go; affection's going to the
        root of things helps
growth; see that early morning light by the
        window sill,
its light touch stimulates more poetry. People
        coming to attend a St. Francis'

prayer have found hope faith charity enough to
   gently really strengthen attention.

WISHING ALL PASSENGERS GOOD HEALTH

The sounds of the not so distant train
   or gods
are like the moods of your poems or
   the colors of
the skies affected by the weather, I just heard
   this rainy Spring day
a not so distant train sound louder than
   usual, as close as
today's greyness and dampness; while sort of waking up
   while reading some
lines concerning transformations by Ovid I knew that our
   means of transportation
go in so many different directions with so many different
   kinds of sleepers, singers,
   in all kinds of weather
   we pray for
   sound health.

A SUBJECT OF MY AFFECTIONS,
PLUS MUSE AND PERSON LOVED

Painters, one with a white beard, one with a black beard,
   and others
are attacking an old red mill, I mean painting a
   subject,
subjecting it to their more or less talent and inevitable
   subjectivity;
you are more or less (some of you may even be bearded)
   attacking this
poem of sorts, sort of subjecting it to your
   individual
enlightenment; at this rate where will we get? at
   any rate

the old dark red mill by the secluded brook and waterfalls and
        shaking leaves
maintains its presence; however the object of my attention
        is never far from you.

NOW IN ALL THE PARTS OF THE WORLD THERE ARE RECEPTIVE WORDS STURDY AND POTENTIALLY GENEROUS

If
all the words that I typed with you, old typewriter,
        could say
farewell, could come like costumed performers on
        an opera stage
the stage would have to be enormous. Would this
        grateful chorus
singing outdo Giuseppe Verdi? no matter; what matters
        is that the thousands
of active words once typed, having travelled somehow
        to you, have
become now and then a part of your voyage; when the
        boat of thought
goes up and down remember some of these actors
        and actresses;
so many people become part of our breathing; the bodies
        swell; the active
tenor and soprano rich in tremulo and giving, beyond
        Addio Addio ! exclamations
of the most personal kind, admit unforgettable thanks
        to the typed libretto.

WHAT FOOLS THESE MORTALS BE

Sometimes I ask
        did I do anything
        or did it all do me
        and therefore do I exist; temporarily
one needs, thinks one needs which is a need, this surname,

this given name, this self-conscious malarkey
about identity and the self. The clams
open and close; the earth mother and moon proceed with tides,
turtles, effective romantic songs;
we take the road not taken but given; we struggle or so it seems
to take, to climax splendidly and
then with Puck we laugh, we in more than Racine excitement feel
we make our rhetoric, our
choices. Then we rejoice that we are part of It as the youth does
riding the waves or Stravinsky
listening to Beethoven.

NO BETTER THAN A WORM,
NOT LESS BRIGHT THAN A GALAXY

What does
the silk worm do?
what does it do for a living? what does it do on
mulberry street?
does it have as many questions as Aristotle?
I think so;
does it have some hesitations in its process of chewing
like cousin Hamlet?
probably; does it achieve early in its life connections with
music of the spheres
like Mozart? I guess so; does it make some noise in the
dark like lovers?
ah yes; does it surprise and leave things to be made of
by others the way
poems do? definitely; did its ancestors help artists
in China and
dress makers in France? fortunately so; can we pray to it and
others as best we can?
we want to.

THE TOTAL PARTLY SPEAKABLE IN A PROLOGUE

Constant companion and
        co-creator
of my misery or joy, sleep
        or awake,
director of desires, at times dramatic
        with disappointments,
unique. Temporal in the soul, and yet
        manifesting It.
The essence of poetry; live unique
        Peter Quince
cannot say what the play is *all* about.
        The sumptuous
process must have its meager moments; the coda
        must have its dragon.

IN THE BEGINNING AND THEREAFTER
THERE WAS NEED FOR SPEECH

Finding a word
is like finding one of the intimate ancestors, one of the
        forefathers, *and*
foremothers someone creatively emphatically added; yes,
        for parents and
children, all the words and legends and true poems past,
        present, and future
came forth to substantiate and help give history and indications
        to our songs. A throng of songs,
a group of religious processions with all the symbols and cymbals
        of necessity came forth
flourishing in a sound and verbal way; so God's ears grew larger.
        A child learned to speak.

WITH INFINITE PLAY, WITH
INFINITE PRESENTATIONS

Loving to communicate,
loving to touch, to see,
to hear, to be active sensible,
loving to touch with his feet
the Divine Ground, to dance,
to read this to you, he
returned often; as often as
sound in waterfalls, as often as
music in the bodies of lovers.

WITHIN AND BETWEEN, ANCIENT AND RECENT

What you can find in me who knows who knows
            if you can
find me; I see myself in part in every object
            subject of the
world I see; there goes the wind, the wordiness; often
            it was the wind
that wafted Psyche or Cupid to Mount Olympos; and
            heavy weight planes
carry all sorts of eccentric passengers many with knapsacks
            to the mountains of
Nepal; the lands of the Imagination we fly to also;
            are you getting away
from me or closer ? holidays will mark our
            climaxes. Some
pilgrims got off a plane and climbed up stairs
            on a cliff in
southwestern China through clouds to a temple. Between
            some carved Chinese
characters you'll find some air—there you've found
            me also.

Each leaf
is responding to the storm, hurricane,
        in its
own way, though there are groups on different
        branches
that sway like a communal Euripidean chorus
        somewhat
hysterical, green universal Dionysian, anyway
        wet and very
agitated, resounding, swishing as the stupendous
        downpour
downpours and I sit and watch the slanted pavement
        of my small
secluded green arbor street become a river, individual
        determined rain drops
hit the pavement; later I'll see, destiny and TV
        permitting, how
the rest of the northeast coast has been battered by
        howling "Hurricane Bob";
the light creating a bright island of light over the
        Notebook I am writing in
flickers; I was trying to read "My Father's Life" by
        Raymond Carver;
I am dry, agitated, my mind listening to the ferocious
        wind; words are so
agitated by all the storms of the self, all the moods of
        every season, every
complex universal moment, my family tree is shaken,
        our fathers' and mothers' and
children's lives so stormed, agitated, uplifted, swirled
        by fears, terrors, needs, delights,
countless troubles. How have we come to these shores
        like wet sailors with
pearls of desires for love ?! O Whitman and other
        Voyagers, *help us*
as we read, write, as we sway on this moving tossing
        vulnerable planet
desiring to bless, searching with undescribable and
        varied commotion
        for love.

YOUR COMMUNION

You mean you want to make a mark on the universe,
        what sort of
mark ? like Mickey Mouse ? like Monkey by
        Wu Cheng-en ?
like the gospel according to St. Mark ? like
        Mark Twain when
he designed his name according to a depth in the
        River of Consciousness ?
like my great teacher Mark Van Doren whose birthday
        will be soon ? his remarks
made us more alive; like John Keats who wrote his name
        on the waters of the world, when
there's a lyrical wave of a very pure order I say John Keats;
        so many names on so many
ever changing waves in the ocean, besides that major matter
        there are galaxies,
Joseph sold in one well arises from another like Ishmael
        or phoenix; here the
generous flame said write your name on my treasured chest;
        whatever we do in
His Light burns like a star; sooner or later the
        travelling light will
        reach its mark.

MODERATION IS NOT A NEGATION OF
INTENSITY, BUT HELPS AVOID MONOTONY

Will you stop for a while, stop trying to pull yourself
        together
for some clear "meaning"—some momentary summary ?
        no one
can have poetry or dances, prayers or climaxes all day;
        the ordinary
blankness of little dramatic consciousness is good for the
        health sometimes,
only Dostoyevsky can be Dostoyevskian at such long
        long tumultuous stretches;
look what that intensity did to poor great Van Gogh ! ;
        linger, lunge,

scrounge and be stupid, that doesn't take much centering
of one's forces;
as wise Whitman said "lounge and invite the soul". Get
enough sleep;
and not only because (as Cocteau said) "poetry is the
literature of sleep";
be a dumb bell for a few minutes at least; we don't want
Sunday church bells
ringing constantly.

THE AFTER SNOWSTORM LANDSCAPE
AND MEMORIES

Network of
many tiny twigs for a moment still then
moving
slightly on the white wall behind my books,
shadows
or sources of song that is, affected by the light
of the early
morning winter dawn after a blizzard. Androscoggin seems
like Antarctica,
the high modulations of white waves in stillness remind
us of large bodies
of Michelangelo, Rodin, Henry Moore; light behind the
slightly shaking
twigs, shadows, network of veins, our lives related to
tree, sun, forest,
Unknown, related to each other and the words in the books
some like Lazarus,
becomes brighter, the little white roof on the postcard of the
Florence Battistero
becomes brighter.

ADDRESSING AN AUDIENCE AS IT
IS DARK AND IT SNOWS

It is good on such a day
to hibernate in poetry.   Bears, can you read the golden and black˙
letters, the emblazoned suns on
the bark of the growing night
inside this mysterious tree ?   Bears,
can you manage when you close your eyes
between syllables and snores to uphold
the worlds ? Bears, can you pretend
you are not growing with poetry
at this very moment ?   Bears, can you
notice how all the trees are trembling with song ?

YOUR THOUGHTS WITH THE
KNOWLEDGE OF SLEEP

Winter skies, how you vary in your
            predictions
of coming snow, predictions of different
            kinds of
silences, skies of nameless tones, un-
    definable
music, you with the saints within the
        clouds, beyond
the clouds, you with your accumulation
        of necessities,
cumulous, numerous. Your skies with the
    knowledge of sheep.

LISTENERS, AUTHORS, OF THE MUSIC

Dancing for the gods—
is there anyone else to dance for ?
yes, but always it is for the gods
        before and behind and

after that particular person; also it's
    not only you
who are dancing but all who came before
    and who needed
the gods; you know neither the gods nor
    the particular
persons perfectly but the communion is
    intact, is in
the river the rhythm the ritual that
    carries you and
your predecessors and future people in need
    and your poems along.

ONE OF THE MANY MARRIAGES OF TRUE MINDS

Mined you. Mind you. Mine.
        You're
mine now and it's about time. Why
        not, I
built you, Great Wall, I made you,
        escape hatch
on the space ship; but escaping's not
        so easy
though we may get out of a hole or walk
        the complete road,
it will take time. We can of course get
        all the gold
or whatever trinkets or yen we claim to
        be valuable.
Mind Spinoza. And take him for a spin
        by the nose.
Knows us ? who knows us after all ? Before
        your fiction
or mind was made up there were plenty of
        other necessities.
The value of the value of a valley gives us
        plenty to explore.
Women too. I implore you and employ you to be
        my priceless mine.

The Robes of Feathers and Flames

FOR THE ATTENTIVE TRANSLATOR

Damp stone
moss covered

if quietly you listen closely enough
you will hear its song

ABANDONED COLUMBIA AMUSEMENT PARK;
NORTH BERGEN, N.J.

There was
night after night in puberty and perplexity and
        something restless
stronger than that which is in all goats, kids,
        keeping me going,
in my dark small bedroom in N.J. opposite
        an Abandoned
Amusement Park (one night its rickety framework
        of wooden skyrocket
which I and a few friends dared to scale at times—
        it all went up in flames
like a dragon dancing), in that room for months
        I was submitted submerged
to dreams (like intimate movies) about miles and
        miles of processions of
nomads and refugees, hordes of very long processions
        in the dark, catacombs
and holocausts and refugees from starvation and wars,
        saw that enacted again
and again and cannibalism, witnessed it as a
        perspiring 11 year old child
in my sleep and the 20th century; why and wherefore ?
        I am still sad thinking of
        the recurring spectacle.

Dragon of Fire, Across from my Night's Window,
Wild cat Meowing to the Skies, collecting stars as if
   they were tickets,
Up and Down the Sex Act Goes, It was across the
   steep street
down which I roller skated down which I whizzed
   on a sled
up which I walked to High School, it was and then
   I saw it Burn
Like the Galaxies in the Making or the Sparks from my
   ever running Desire
expressed in future future Krishnas, Was Is
   Amusement Park,
Lark made of Evening and Ferris Wheels and Whips and a
   Crowded Swimming Pool
Made of Electric Lights and Banners, One Night as
   in an Illumination
opposite my window (and in that room I dreamed all
   fears, all gardens, all adventures,
   all murders, all dances, all prayers)
the Sky Rocket or as it is called by some the Roller Coaster
   like a vast up and down Dragon Wiggling
   like All Joy
Was all on Fire and as I had watched asleep and
   awake lives, races, stars,
   worlds, processions,
I now Watched It Saying Shiva Shiva Shiva
   When You Dance
   These Events are Mentioned.
Acrobats dove out of the sky like Giotto's Angels
   and I told the secret sharer
   in the Priest's Games
You, Reader, do not be afraid, your children will
   have such windows to Mythologies.
Now Now Now, Lover, Dance out of existence the wars and fears.
   The tears of fire turned like ferris wheels.

EVERY DEATH IS THERE AT
THE BEGINNING OF TIME

What was it like
when they first saw the first dead body ?
can we   who conceived it   speak of it now ?

       was it like a parent not answering a child ?
       was it like a parent not present when desired ?
when they and their children tried to talk to it
       and it could not answer
when they and their children and we asked it to stand
       and to move   as we ask the poem to move
       or music to be heard from trees and stones
       as in newness it always was heard
       before our first death

they and we
       do we remember
who had seen God walk by the lion and the lamb
       by the trees and the sun and moon
perhaps
       kept saying   it is not true   it is not true
       this mouth must breathe
       this hand must touch with love
       as God touched Adam and Eve

what was it like when the first lost children saw
       their first lost parents dead ?

RAIN

The cemetery holds the rain, receives the rain,
the night street, the many leaves,
the hands of children, the eyes of the dead,
    the heads of birds,
receive the rain, the land and Word
receive the rain, the darkness is the rain,
the rain is the darkness, the daily life of
sadness receives the rain, the dark coming
of winter, the quietness of death,

receives the rain,
the sick in the hospital see the rain
on the windows,
the lost or angry children see the rain
on their hands,
see the rain on the face of the land, see
the rain in the eyes of the sky, see the
night in the breathing of the darkness.

THE DEFORMATION SOCIETY

The city is like
a fragment of a large dirty useless ugly machine
some Agent of part of man's insanity that
we will call Deformation,
vestigial and deformed men and women have built their
machines to wander around in it,
occasionally they come out of their cars or banks or
department stores or plastic bags
and regurgitate and twist and turn or jog, while eating out of
their plastic bags in the Parking Lot
surrounded by Automobile Exhaust and Acid Rain they turn on
the little machine which tells them of
terrorists, dentures, and the
failure of energy,
the governments accumulate the over-kill, the nuclear waste
is weirdly and at great expense
and madness stored away
to contaminate the grandchildren; and so you wearily proceed
in the Waste Land.

DETERMINATION IN THE NATION
DETERMINATION IN THE NATION

isn't it enough
isn't it enough
always to be running to be running to be running
to be running to be running to be running to be running

266

from what to what to be running to be keeping in shape
so to speak so to run to be running isn't it enough to be
always keeping in shape doing it every day to be running what for
no you are convinced it is good for you it is great it is greater
just doing that to be running why not since there is no place to stop
no place to see no place to really love no place no place
do I not hear myself speak to myself over and over and over again
        no one else
as I run as I am running as I am running as I am running

DO YOU NOT SEE THE CHILD WEEPING
BEHIND THE CLOUD ?

Why   why
why   do you cry
caterpillar on the leaf
repeating to me my mother's grief,
there in the palms of the hands, there in the
     pain in the feet
why   why   all those crucifixion scenes ? they
     cannot be erased,
the dead soldier in the thought of the mother,
     it was beating in my heart,
why   why   Cain in chains, the blood on the child,
     as the world turns,
as Hiroshima burns, it is burning still, it
     is there forever
burning in the bones of the child and parent, the shadow
     forever on the stone,
the shadow of that plane that carries the bomb.
     And now the numb
the lost prepare more bombs, here   everywhere,
     more missiles more bombs
     to destroy genesis
the mystery of all generations, more bombs   more missiles
     for advanced madness,
advanced absolute lostness and sadness, more more
     more need to destroy
     the self the world,
when there is so much love at the roots of words of plants
     this end of April day   why   why
     lost man   do you wish to die ?

What good would it do them—
if I became ritualistic and bowed in my poems
    to every
survivor of Hiroshima and to all the dead, to the
    shadow
on the stone that has become part of my shadow, to
    those with
cancer at length suffering and dying ? I would like to
    do some good
but I continue to be stunned and feel the great painful
    deprivation
that separated them from me. I know that I belong to
    them more than to
    any country.

PARENT/SEER AND ANSELM KIEFER'S TREE OF JESSE AND OTHER SCENES

Father with child (delicate sensitive blooming father
    with child sleeping)
looking at and surrounded by the vast scenes of terror
    and devastation,
the Tree of Jesse bombed again and again and again and again
    and the mother and father
and child dismembered, tortured, thrown to the ashes of
    Europe,
Die Meistersinger, der Ubermensch, every kindness and
    every child
murdered and blasphemed by Mein Kampf, and so
    the agonies
are not understood, and so the Wailing Wall and the
    Crucifixion
are not understood and so the Jewish child and so
    Edith Stein
are taken to the concentration camps, all of
    Germany's
spiritual heroes blasphemed, and every soul in
    every individual's body:
    all nations.

THE BOOK

The words of the Book may burn
the Book at the center of the Holocaust may burn
but the Original Book will not burn
it returns like the ghost of Hamlet's Father
it returns like Lazarus from his winding sheet
it returns from every drop of blood in every concentration camp
it returns from the bodies and bones of all those heaped in
      all the concentration camps
it returns from the silence of the frightened children
it grows larger and larger like the voice of Hamlet's Father
it comes out of the desolation of the mouths of the starving
it comes from the ashes of all of the waste land
the hunger artist in his almost endless night is desiring it
the secret scribe in his ascendancy is preparing to find
      the indestructible word in
      the indestructible Book

I SEE THE TIRED FACES, I SEE THE PLACES
EVERYWHERE ASSIGNED FOR MURDER

I once
read a story "The Penal Colony"
by that brave one that bold one that old testament
      scribe for me and many,
I don't remember the details; but now I think of
      many in the dark sitting
for hours and hours, for years it seems in some kind
      of waste and exhaustion,
watching TV, not in an electric chair which would
      do the job quick
but in an arm chair receiving night after night
      instead of the dreams
"messages from the gods" and Homer and Kafka, being
      imprinted everywhere
on the body by the vibrations from the TV machines,
      the messages from
the commercials and the anchor men about lies, deficits,
      disasters; the decaying
goes on slowly; as the ambitious here, there, and everywhere practice

their golf and diplomacy,
build up the military mechanisms for murder, the chemistry
        of warfare is taking place
inside, outside; the streets are a disaster; the very air we breathe
        contaminated, the poor suffer;
try on your gas mask; the body is being made to flicker
        to flounder to shake in
sickness or staleness; patriotic phrases between commercials are sent
        out to accompany
those in their helmets and with instruments of destruction; do you not see?
        invaders against the soul,
you with your commercial smiles and pretence at benevolence that
        you too—that everyone—
        Everyone Suffers.

FIRE AND ICE   FROZEN SUFFERING
    GIACOMETTI PROPHECY

        Barren stage
        post holocaust stage
        post nuclear war barren place
        faceless victims   extended shadows

THE SUICIDES

        Why did they want to leave this earth,
                the young ones ?
        not even they know; what sickness of the
                temporary self
        wanted them to leave dew, dawn, plum,
                grapes, the breeze
        on the cheek, the sea spray on the body, the
                sayings of elated Keats ?
        no one knows; the heart ache and the more than thousand
                natural shocks
        everyone knows, pre-Adam, pre-individual birth,
                of the turtle carrying
        its world, of Christ carrying his cross. They have separated

270

themselves from their shadows
and the sun and us; we could list the procession, intimate
acquaintances, others; the
pool of blood is very large over which we speak unanswered
but known underground.

MISUNDERSTANDINGS MAKE FOR HOLOCAUST

Are there dead letters? dead letters, dead soldiers,
voices of lovers
who try to reach the person they love, and yet
often it seems
the letters do not arrive, and so Juliet dies and
so Bartleby
prefers not to eat. Too late, too soon; confusion
in the mortal
Post Office; all the dead bodies in Hiroshima; all
the dead letters
taken to be burned; the cremation ground. And so
King Lear turns
in the wheel of fire. And so St. Joan is burned on
the pyre. The pilot
is lost in densest fog, no voice, no light,
no desire for life.

". . . TRA LA PERDUTA GENTE . . ."

The fact that many angels could dance on a pin
didn't interest him
or that phoenixes could change their color and
always remain
essentially golden and flame as they rose, or that
all the biological
facts are all marvels and profound mysteries and
can be completely
thought out only by God, that each sand was a
grain of eternity,
that Blake was on the scene when the tiger was made,

that did no
longer interest the lost man or the very lost
people; the
surprising news of Dante was still ever changing
and frightening
and true: "they had lost the good of the intellect."

IN UTTER QUIETNESS MAKE YOUR IMPONDERABLE CHOICE

The Ancient Tree
in a stupendous storm, hurricane,
was behaving like an octopus in a frenzy;
Shiva could not be so wild or so elephantine;
not behaving "properly"; scaring the neighbors,
        the police,
the fire departments; *where* are the birds finding
        protection ?
it is summer and the students are not present,
        otherwise they and
their computers might be blown away; what we
        learn from this
howling, this twisting, this fierceness, this uncontrollable
        Nature remains
to be seen if anything remains to be seen tomorrow
        morning; I think
of poor King Lear and his Fool and all the foolish
        battered rest of us.
Branches break from trees, divorces and death take place.
        For many centuries
all over the world tribes have huddled in fear; Ahab
        and Job rage and
Questions remain unanswered; but everyone is drenched,
        many drowned,
processions of bewildered refugees from all over the world
        in darkness
suffer, send out messages. The howling of children and
        leaves, of twisted
branches increases; I try to find the quiet at the
        eye of the storm,
the I of Buddha's everywhere and nowhere. While you can
        ponder the whirling

of elemental dervishes. Dread and all philosophies
      and little huts
blasted; the Fool's hat flies into the vast dark;
      did he say
octopus ? not one but hundreds in heavy and fast moving
      violence gone berserk.
Choose what you can to worship, word or toy, some
      memory of kindness;
someone you love; pray to that; hold on, hold on;
      rejoice as you shiver that you
      make your peaceful choice.

ADJUST, ADJUST ! — ETERNITY
TO THE TEMPORAL FIRE

You have rattled, cried, and despaired in the universe, you have
      seen shooting stars,
you have seen fish and birds and more miracles, you have heard
      from Adam and Eve, you have
murdered King Duncan and burned on the Night of Fire with Pascal,
      you have spoken to the green wall,
you have heard from the green fire, you have cried and despaired
      and wandered as the universe adjusted to you.
You have seen children born with your name and you have wondered
      who you are; the leaves have said listen; the fish have said listen,
      the children have said listen; learning the alphabet
you begin to spell Eden; you cry as you see the blood of the King;
      the star that came to the window
      waits for your word.

MASTER   BEFORE AND AFTER
THE NAMING AND ALL LANGUAGES

Sometimes
in winter
here in the icy or slushy North
it seems as if your soul is carrying
      your body

a load as it gets older   I won't
    try to define that
Thing   it's been miraculous, its instincts, its molars,
    its liver, all its
functions which have their (interrelated ?) fine complexities
    for scientists, doctors,
to study   already you know that it's better than
    any Anatomy Lesson
could suggest   but as you get some arthritis bursitis
    lumbago   as one eye
sees more and more blurred   you saw the Taj Mahal !
    you   at least   at times
pity and laugh   poor dear body,   and think again with fire
    Light   or   sunrise
where we began   you soul had the weightless strongest
    easiest at its freest
strength to perceive and Be the sun as it is Rising   to
    see   receive   and Be
the sun as it is blazing orange red beyond the mountains
    before and after
all thought   lighter   as it is upholding and letting go
    every body

DECEMBER

A train is passing in the snowy distances—
    if I told the hardware facts
    about what it is probably carrying
    it might be a depressing train of thought,
    nuclear waste, the future to be wasted
    forever, the present contaminated;
    the built-in obsolescence of our
    mechanical gadgets and our grim
    and decrepit Mechanical World;
I heard the train whistle and it started that 20th century fear;
    I realize that if Jacob Boehme
    were the train conductor and
    he were going to Robert Bly
the snowy distances and different voices of light nearby would
    reveal their angels.

WHO WILL ASSUME TO CONTINUE THE FABLE
THAT EVERY ONE BEGAN WRITING

After the deluge the chipmunk asserts its small head; will
        there be 3, 4, 5 after the holocaust ?
not bugs, divine as they and we all are, not chipmunks,
        will coyness and speed have any value ?
but people, unique, worthy of Shakespeare, malicious, stupid,
        self-destructive, occasionally
slightly constructive as we all are. Either/or. Awe. The
        Taj Mahal gone to the N.J. dump
into the international nuclear holocaust. So Dante's Hell
        will seem like a charred paperback, a cinder
in the cremation ground, fools and sorts of lovers, murderers
        and more fools in ashes; will there
be a question of To Be ? "My little fool is hanged". . . all,
        all babies and people of the most driving kind,
        and Venice and Mozart and Monet could be
all gone, all blasphemed, in a moment. I am speaking . . . of
        you-and-me; if we are interrupted by the
        overkill that we have been a long
        time and a long crime Preparing
who will finish the sentence ? who will hold the baby towards
        the Light ?

LIKE 14 TINY DISCIPLES OF ST. VALENTINE

I suspect
that if I held those tiny 14 ducklings in my hands
        they would seem
to weigh less than a few feathers yet those 14 hearts
        would be beating with
the ardor of what made the galaxies and the collected operas
        of Verdi plus quacks
of all kinds; familiar with the secret thoughts of the
        Mother, familiar with water
and weeds and whatever wonders are in their elements,
        skies, fish, clouds, bees,
reflections as their unseen feet paddle. What made the
        thoughts of Plato go ?
What made the poems of Emily show ? something better

than pearls drops from
our feathers as we all shake as we all begin to
continue and to fly.

PRACTICAL CONCERNS CONTINUE

It's been figuring itself (and us) out and
          in for
billions of light (and dark) years; and now and
          then some
daring person dabs a bit or gabs, dabs some
          chiaroscuro,
or says damn it I can't understand much of it
          or you or me,
better say bless it. The nearby mother duck with
          17 attending ducklings
sitting on the grass, 18 miracles of them, near the pond,
          opens her long beak
silently several times and via body language indicates
          like the Bhagavad-Gita
that I should mind my own business. She's deliberately and
          universally protective;
bless it; the ducks, the flying birds, the quacking, the early
          morning coolness,
my and your limited rationality; put it in its religious place.
          The ripples, the light,
in motion on the pond and on the mother duck's wings
          are useful.

THE QUACKING, GREEK EURIPIDEAN OR
LOCAL ANDROSCOGGIN, OR OTHERWISE

It may not sound "poetic" or high noble to your
          ears or desire,
tragedy has many many sounds, unique
          personal as
always as joy; this almost constant quacking
          of the mother duck

followed by her hurrying 5 ducklings as she searches
        here, there, everywhere
in the early morning pond for the missing
        6th duckling; that
miniature deity we saw last night in the
        company with his crew.
Where are you this morning ? the mother asks in
        different tones, in
essential grief, of the son killed in Vietnam or
        El Salvador or
the Italian village or the Palestinian homeless place
        and on to everywhere
in the world at war. Wars too need not be
        imagined as epic or
political meaningful, there are everywhere familiar
        separations, disasters;
Cain changes his masks countless times through all
        the centuries. The
mother grieves as she searches as she cannot find
        her son in the street or
        the pond or the grave.

THE ROBES OF FEATHERS

They had spent a lot of time those more than
        40 ducks
during various seasons and different times of
        light and dark
cloudiness or moon light or bright sun or
        windiness
quacking and so forth and yesterday as I
        walked around
the pond looking for their beauty, their
        waddling or gliding
or pretty behind up in the air as the head
        was under water fishing
or as they rose as some sort of mythological
        ancient bird
stretching the neck and spreading the fabulous
        wings—I noticed
they were gone. Flown to another life, another
        light, a warm South;

and today I wonder does that water of the pond
          on which they lived and
played for so long somehow feel different;
          maybe not; does the mirror
hold the image of the actor? it is only foolishly
          temporarily sad that
the reflections of gestures of lovers and our poems
          are written on the
          waters of the world.

HOMAGE TO THE HUMUS WHICH NOURISHES THE FUGUES OF BACH

Were you afraid to look at his death, his shut eyes, his color ?
          thinking of your own death, thinking of the
          plant or planet's death ?
it is all one thing; no it was him, though I averted my eyes
          from the body of his closed eyes,
his lightest of lightest delicate body dim green, dim grey,
          our way of prayer is
dim and lightest of light, the fragile temporary small bird
          dead on our porch,
at 1st I thought it was a leaf, and then the grief of that
          perfection which is unique
made me wonder; now the wonder that can no longer fly
          like all our civil war brothers
joins the humus of the turning world; the flying solar system
          temporary; brother of
the lightest of the light, when I lift you from the porch
          there seems to be no weight
though I am grave, you of the many songs prepared for by
          millions of years
and brother to the leaf and to any person entering or
          leaving this world.

IN MOURNING AND IN HOPEFUL PRAYER
AFTER A TREMENDOUS STORM

The birds, many flying fast this
      after the storm
      morning,
must wonder where did their ancestral temples go,
      those trees destroyed
      uprooted
by the fiercest lightning storm a week ago; the campus
      maintainers, those pastoral
      attentive heroes
sawed the rest away; today a few chunks of huge reminders,
      remainers here in battered
      Maine;
we try to maintain our homes, our education, our
      fragile branches of life, leaves,
      poems
places for birds and songs, and suddenly a gale, a wail, a
      disaster, a fiercest twister
      accompanied
by lightning flashes wrecks a grandfather, some ancient priests;
      hands in shreds, after tons of
      tears,
we beg the elements and the mind of Man to be kind to future children
      and future nests, forthcoming
      birds.

WHILE WORMS ARE BURROWING
IN THE DAMP CATACOMBS

Long
silver
slightly curved fish,
in the noisy narrow grey silver stream,
brook, crucifix in my book, of the damp wet
      grey morning,
here on this short new bridge, new testament, as I see
      you dead below,
as I see and hear the long white silver commotion of
      the narrow slightly

curved, slightly zig-zagging, ever murmuring waterfalls,
        I wonder,
I explore, exploit, a gospel, mysterious as it is
        recurring;
I take recourse in words, they flow by, I insist on a
        temporary
wet meaning; the silver swimmer dead like the babbling brook
        keeps our larger eternal
        truth somewhat
        undecipherable.

RELIGIOUS SUBSCRIBERS

The bat found dead lying on the porch
        like a
small priest on its side, frozen during
        the night
when we were all below zero, we heard
        its sounds
in the night, we thought it was in our
        bed room,
put on the light, looked around, but no
        no sign of him,
but our fear kept us from sleeping, he
        must have been
outside trying to get in, and now I feel terrible
        and guilty, I feel
like a murderer, I felt sorry for the little
        frozen priest;
I reason too simply that he should stay in his
        house, and know
I never hated him; but fear and guilt are as large
        as the night.

WHAT SIGNALS BEYOND THE RADAR
HAVE BROUGHT US TOGETHER?

Little blind brother,
small ash, black folded paper wings,
      tiny
as petals of a flower burned, small brother
      seeking
for food and escape from the underground,
      and all
you lost and in prisons, and all souls
      frightened
starved or charred by life; tiny dead
      bat that
I found in my cellar, this is my frail
      requiem for you.

THE UNDERGROUND PRESSURE

He seemed so plump, furry, plunked down, as if sinking slowly
      into the ground, resigned to humus, still
      as one of God's words that died,
his curve of fur, his small mound of monument, I found the
      precious beast behind the tree,
carried there by some growling dog ? come there to die ?
      chuck chuck said the fates and
      the smell of his death
came to us now and then; I stare and I gasp, my mind cannot grasp
      his nature though I am soul brother
to this brown and black brother, small woodchuck; the vulture flies
      are at Kilimanjaro;
I chant my Gregorian make-up; I make up prayers for the occasion;
      a long armed spade digs a hole,
      I carry him in a pail,
when I lift him on the spade he is as light as a moth;
      the fate of all galaxies;
pious Rilke with his own scent says "be conversant with
      transformation"; Orpheus   Orpheus
      you take us underground.

WHAT POSITIONS DO THEY AND WE ASSUME
IN THE ENCAPSULATED STILLNESS ?

While
somewhere in a capsule deep in the sea
      off the Florida coast
seven visitors to the earth who planned to
      visit outer space
lie dead with their advanced technological gadgets
      and once active
mysterious eyes, all kinds of scientists and many
      argumentative committees
discuss in details the possible causes of the Challenger's
      explosion, flaming
demise into fish wandering seas. Octopus nearby,
      and dead sea captains,
ships like old cultures gone to the bottom. The many
      slightly alive
statisticians argue and probe and computers they think
      are at their advanced
command. How silent they are, the sky dreamers, those
      children in the womb
      of the metal.

DO NOT DEFACE YOUR RELATIVE'S IMAGE

Staged;
who shall be executed ? who shall be a slave ? who
      shall be tortured ?
do it quickly, impulsively, or take all the time you want,
      it will happen
with all variety of devices and vices through the centuries
      in what some call
high or low places; who shall be deprived, who shall
      be raped, who shall
be misrepresented ? there is Christ presented to the public;
      here is Anne Frank
in hiding. None can escape the suffering. Face it as you
      must face yourself;
face it with the artist's skill, face it with the saint's
      compassion; place

it before all crowds, before your secret privacy, so all
      love's integrity here
      Is Mankind.

THE FEVER AND BLOOD AND THE ACHES
AND PAINS IN EVERYMAN'S GOLDEN LEGEND

They had their troubles, those saints,
      St. Sebastian with all those arrows stuck in him,
      St. Apollonia with her teeth out,
      St. Lorenzo grilled,
saints hatcheted and tortured in a variety of ways natural
      to the sad masochism and sadism of man,
but they would be the 1st to say—pity pity mankind,
      so many with years of arthritis and cancer
      and other forms of drawn out
      physical irritation or agony,
the wheel of diseases crushes often slowly so many, we see
      the pale and spent on their
      hospital beds
struggling to breathe, desiring sleep and relief from pain,
      so many
the saints and good nurses know. Job and King Lear
      carrying their
Bedlam with them say patience patience as the
      lightning strikes again.

A NOT INSIGNIFICANT SMALL PART
OF A GREAT FABLE

      My heart goes out to them
            to Gregor Samsa
            to Mme. Bovary
            to that bewildered Hamlet
and so I am extended, and so we are dramatized, as a
            matter of planetary motion,
            we turn together, we
make a show of it, the burning solar system, the

familiar mysterious connections,
we palpitate with sea anemones and grand Italian opera,
as a matter of
very complex intimate very fabulous fact it is one heart
that we are lyrically
a part of.

IN INTANGIBLE TIME

Strangers
we are such strangers to each other

we wonder what processions
over the Himalayas led to our
ancestors and their

hard working ancestors who ate, slept,
looked up at the unreachable
moon, you are not

reachable, and I am a scattered
mystery to myself
year after year.

ORBIT AND CHARISMA AND ORIGIN

Lost lost lost, it's been going on for centuries,
for millennia ? this
feeling that I, that you, that they have lost something,
Joseph in Egypt,
Christ at the last supper, Keats in his Odes, so many
millions in Ohio or
Indonesia or anywhere, lost ? lost a world that we
came from ? lost
a world that we dream of going to ? why ? underneath
the business, the sporting,
this element of something missing ? What is it we imagine
we have not

Completed ? not United ? So we go on a secret mission
        unknown to ourselves
occasionally emitting some sperm, some poems, some maps
        for new voyages;
Dulcinea, is it Dulcinea ? Elysian fields with Wordsworth's
        daffodils ? anyway
you look at it through the centuries, sighing or searching or
        causing trouble or
tourism no doubt we are somewhat daffy; shaking at
        least slightly
to get into orbit; to find Penelope; to find Hermione;
        resourceful persisting
            to find the Origin.

                        *

    It's where there is
            where there's no desire for words,
    that's sad, but saying it's sad even flatly
    is getting close to a saving grace, a memory,
    memory of events somewhat carried by words, by
    the force that made the desire for speech, speech
    may be pedestrian but it bears some memory of song,
    song is where the full body is with soul, you can feel its
    light expand; when the wide sun rises
            we know the prologue can be enlightening.

HART CRANE, MANY MUSICIANS,
    RELIGIOUS ARCHITECTS,
MANY DEMOCRATIC CHORUSES, ETC.

    Taking
    to heart Hart Crane who took to heart Hopkins,
            Swinburne, Eliot, Christopher Columbus,
    Shelley, Shakespeare, America, Whitman Of Course
            and all his other lovers,
    building the Bridge with him along with them
            we learn to be lavish, learn

285

to give and give, to splurge, to urge Rhetoric for
        All its worth, sending our
lyrics to the sea gulls, diving into chaos and
        the sea, and furthermore
giving sound constructive Reverence and Sense. I sense
        your needs, our needs,
I sense Reverberations of the Mystic Synthesis,
        I see Melville in his
nobility and rage by our side; anonymous readers
        and lovers crossing the
Bridge, we begin once more the hope, the exuberance
        of the Everchanging Energy Giving
        Resounding New World Symphony.

A MONTH OF MANY BIRTHDAYS AND MUCH FOG

A foggy day and I am sequestered, secluded, requested
        by my poetry
to write; so after early morning coffee and in ubiquitous
        dampness it feels
cozy right here by the bright light of my long desk
        and 65 year old life.
You do what you can to clarify, to define with some
        affectionate regard
so called thought coming out of consciousness, coming
        out of what
shall we call it? ay, that's the question that makes
        philosophy out of
so long life; the slanted street with its few remaining
        autumn leaves
is wet; the frequent active alert squirrels so far are
        in seclusion.
And you, unknown and secluded reader, as I imagine you
        sounding these
phrases out, are called to my attention; such undisturbing company
        pleases me.

SEARCHING, FINDING, LOSING, REMAKING
THE DISCOVERY; SEARCHING, FINDING

The looks
of the hands change, the looks of the arms,
     the looks of
the belly, the looks of the eyes, and under the
     eyes and
under the changed hair and body what has
     changed ?
hard to name; the images in the mirrors
     more changeable
than the moon; the photographs burn like
     autumn leaves;
inseparable from the cosmos and all time that
     created the
second, that created the appearing and disappearing
     sky diver, sea
diver; the divinations divide us in millions;
     and yet we know
within the Burning Bush the ancestors and
     our selves are
as alive as every flaming sun; the daughters of
     the Water and the Night
     wander.

THE LATE AFTERNOON GROUND COVERED
WITH MONTHS OF SNOW

Patient
leafless tree
all winter in the world of snow
     as the
sundial casts its varying shadows,
     firm rooted
deep rooted in earth and necessity, you
     keep your
private life gather what life you can
     into your
trunk until we're drunk with the full summer
     splendor of

your abundant leaves. Now in my Library chilliness
        I see the
dark shadows of buildings on both sides of you and
        you centered
in my admiration tall ample patient receiving the
        sun's light.

RELATED TO SONNET 29

When consciousness seems dead like a snake that will
        not move,
when after days of mugginess, routine, fear, disappointments,
        "the thousand natural shocks
that flesh is heir to," when there's post crisis-futility,
        the body is just responding
but consciousness does not grow like the sap in the tree or
        the genius in the Archangel Michael,
one shoves Hamlet aside and says to him or some other street man
        "make room for me."
There's always a little bit of Lazarus left in one's sense of humor.
        But the prison despondency
in the grave days when phoenix is just a small dictionary word
        almost makes you not hear
the underground rivers when sutras and Gregorian chants 1st receive
        their temporal beginnings.
Then your body in my mind appears beginning some of its music
        and my consciousness is charmed
        like the swaying snake in
        the cosmic basket.

THE FATHER EDUCATED BY
THE LONG GONE SON

In the
tunnel I am returning to often
after my daily work and night work too
        at my desk composing music
searching for my son, finding on the wall of the

long long tunnel,
       zig zagging or curving at times, anyway as natural
              as the shapes of rocks,
       Altamira, Lascaux, Puente Viesgo, wherever, I find
              signs of hands, fingers outspread,
      small drawings of ponies, monuments of bisons,
              migrations of horses,
      rivers and voices . . . when I recall in different ways
              I am surprised to hear
      this saint or that deer, the bibles of underground rivers
              are reminding him
              to remind me,
      I live by the clover, I burn by the fern, I turn the
              mandala and sparks
              fly in my hands,
      I note here is music that fish will understand, here is
              a course for the beginning of time.

REMEMBERING AN INCIDENT IN A VILLAGE IN THE MOUNTAINS NEAR THE CENTER OF SICILY

Nothing quite
      satisfying? fulfilled?
      this poem, those thousands, my life?
I wake up this chilly damp drizzling end of May
      morning in Maine and
wonder where I am, what is Missing, who knows
      what is going on, where
we are; we know how far from the truth those are
      who take the census, who
psychoanalyze; and in the doldrums and dampness and
      with a general sense of loss
of foresight, insight, the ecstatic vision you slightly
      imagine Quixote folded up.
The bazaar of Xanadu or Araby seems commercial or
      sort of closing;
you remember in Calatafimi Christ on a mule
      riding into Jerusalem
amidst the parked cars and the somewhat stunned people.
      Everyman seen
by the Mystery and witnessed in eternity a bit battered by
      time and amidst the

automobile exhaust nevertheless even in untheatrical ordinary
        old clothes and
admitting our shortcomings, distractions, doubts
        ventures adventures to
stunned believed in, as we see Christ once more on
        Palm Sunday ride in
on a mule, somehow to go towards that annual eternal
        event of Easter.

WHO IS THE ONE WHO SEEMS TO HAVE LOST A MILLION TIMES BUT ALWAYS WON

Who is the challenger
who is the heavy weight champion
        if he wants to be
who is the shyest who can be the boldest
        if he must be
who is the darkest who can be as bright as a
        star when all's right
who is the defender of the faith who can laugh at all
        religions respectfully
who is the flyer who can go through death and return
        with you and some poems
who is the promoter of celestial industries right here
        on the common ground
who is the untiring one who can walk in the snow and
        see flowers for you
who is astounded and astounded and awakened by the love
        the earth gave you and me
        and the next reader.

SACRED STONE AND UNPREDICTABLE HEIGHTS

It depends what rock we run up against
        and then
the water will turn to spray, to fountain,
        to Christ,
to christen the light in terms of all mortal

air and
hardness. We say we believe in necessary leaps
or detours
to continuation. The personal and natural lyricism needs
such flexibility;
some said He moved a rock as only death and He
could do
completely. In this natural life of ours with obligations
and obstacles
difficulties remain hard; our gentleness and faith will
do what can
be done for momentary miracles; I see the Sun,
the rainbow,
in that spread of enlightening spray as it touches
what makes us
leap and sing.

THE RESEARCH PROCESSION ADVANCES

Fingering the texts
the Dead Sea Scrolls become alive,
the fossils from deepest sea design
the sides of high mountains; decide if you can
the notes coming from the fan shape of the sea shell,
millions of ancestors before your grandchild's grandchild
had them in mind; human continuity is long, including the
Hero with a million faces, Shiva of the many arms and legs,
and Shakespeare of the many poems; and yet we know
that in a twinkling of an eye, in the fall of a sparrow,
it can disappear. So Herodotus gives his respect.
Histories and archeologists and all artists, priests,
continue their praise-research.

THE SUPPLY OF INFINITY

Sometimes
it is difficult to live
in such a way that what needs

to be transformed into a poem will be
      transformed,
what needs to be left out must strongly
      be left out
so that the original in our being has some
      light, has enough
force purity to keep us somewhat going in and
      towards that
insistent secure realm we came from, the
      only security
the inexhaustible gift of that Absolute. It is
      easy for the
next poem to want to survive and to have it want
      you to survive
      shine forth.

THE MOST ACCESSIBLE INACCESSIBLE

We must be secretive invisible in
      giving
a token or as private as possible in
      a crowd,
giving a sprig of lilac to the altar, a
      note to
the invisible most intimate god; all
      currencies
of the soul are rich like this, golden beyond
      all knowledge,
all exchange of wealth of this kind makes us
      invulnerable
to chance, to loss; the exchange of faithful
      vows; the
most private thought, the greatest need, before the
      beginning of all poems.

AFTER HEARING OF THE DEATH
OF ANDRÉS SEGOVIA JUNE 2, 1987

How many nights have I heard you,
>   guitarist,
>   Segovia,
seeker and finder of the sound at the heart of water,
>   at the heart of jasmine, hibiscus,
>   at the moment of birth and death,
how many times for me have you made time resound, tones
>   of our deepest thoughts, of our
>   most essential desires,
fingering, listening, pausing, quietly, as precisely as
>   absolute care can be ?
and so while we wept or dreamt or felt at one with the world,
>   Alhambra or Bach,
you brought to me the night with its flowers and fountains
>   once more purified and human
>   to the perfected sentience,
>   reverence, soul.

UNFINISHED ACHE OR ALL THE PEOPLE IN ALL
OF THE NURSING HOMES, MILLIONS OF
PEOPLE ON CITY STREETS OR IN LONELINESS

Now
some people always have some sort of arrow
>   stuck in them—
(I had 2 teeth taken out weeks ago and am still
>   aching)—maybe
because of arthritis, bursitis, *etc.*; let the doctors
>   list all the names,
we feel the pains. As a young boy near Lake Como
>   I remember
many images of saints, one with a bleeding knee
>   and a stone,
all sorts of obvious inflictions, Sant' Apollonia
>   martyred by having
all her teeth taken out (without novocaine);
>   anyway as
Romeo who was soon to be wounded along with

his friends said
of Mercutio, "He jests at scars that never felt a wound";
    and Roethke said
(today's his birthday) "Love is not love unless
    love's vulnerable."

MARCH BLIZZARD

A thin and crippled and sweet and humorous
very old man dying, on his winter bed,
in an oxygen tent, very very thin, Irish,
such a good Yankee craftsman, ascetic,
bachelor, dreamy philosophic; a few weeks ago
he climbed a thin ladder to take some snow
and ice off the roof, boyish up there he worked,
clear; now in the painted hospital he tries
to breathe; the whole wide day is dim
with heavy snow, it is still snowing; a dying
whale in the vast sea comes up several times
for air; what angels are ready ?
                        And *then*
fooling all the predictions of the doctors and charts
and tremulous fears of his brother and sisters
(they adore him, and one had a permanent-wave
just to be ready in case)—and then he came out
of the hospital, went down to the grocery store
to see some friends; and recently
                        he's been on
                        the roof again !

FABERGÉ DECORATED WITH THE MEDAL
OF THE LEGION OF HONOR
(THE RICHMOND MUSEUM, VIRGINIA)

        The Czar
        for a while
        was preciously
        persistent;

294

Czar Alexander the 1st
gave his wife an
egg of gold and jewels;
Czar Alexander the 2nd
gave his wife an
egg of diamonds and other jewels;
the last Czar gave his
wife some diamond eggs
and that was the end of that.

The extraordinary
ordinary chicken
laid an egg
and from then on
Easter was everywhere,
chickens galore were
for the extraordinary
ordinary folks; a
new hen was born;
this is not politics
but poultry and poetry.
Our fine feathered friends
are cackling by farms.
Mysteries continue like
chickens, like extraordinary
ordinary productive poems.

THE WORLD SURROUNDED BY MUCH SPACE; INSIDE A SEA SHELL DISTANT ECHOES

Sometimes
late at night
sitting up you sit only with your papers
    and things that
seemed alive in the photographs seem very distant,
    anyway there is
a vast silence, sentiments that you thought made
    meaning seem
to have slid away; you know there are bundles
    of letters
from the past; you see some buddhas in
    introspection;

you're wrong about it, everything in the room has
    a life but
for a while you are separated. The tide has receded
    and there
isn't much motion but underneath the lives of
    all your
sentiments you realize as you write there is a
    breathing, there
    is a life.

GIVE HEED AND HEAT TO THE HEROIC

Now that I've found you
        and winter will come,
        kindling wood, be kind;
begin to give us warmth; today I'll make you small,
        so that you will make the
        fire large; small ·
beginnings enlarge our virtue, fire our enthusiasm,
        make cozy the house,
protect Rosey from the cold. To stir a light
        is necessary thankful enterprise.
Would that we could on cold or grim or grey days
        all be kind; the kind
that Emerson would cheer; and Whitman shaking the
        flakes of snow from his white beard
says: "Here is the hospitality which forever indicates heroes."

INDEPENDENTLY APPROACHING
ORIGINAL SPONTANEITY

Whistling what some might call an insipid tune, the stranger,
        common, democratic, for a moment
is as happy as a lark; from the dark a moment of freedom
        is summoned, it is approaching summer
both made and not made by him, the ambling descendent of Adam
        and sun and Whitman, for a
moment what made Chaucer clear is clear in his tune and he

whistles away
as free as any more than national bird, at this moment he has
        heard the invocation from the everywhere
Word and sings it back to the face of light, the brightest day
        accompanies him and then
things slip, slide, slush, crumble, chaos into the old
        slime, morbid thoughts inside the worm,
the world and his consciousness re-enact cancer and pollution;
        the dark is all murky and Poe is at his morbid piano
playing tunes about the disintegration of the psyche. Young people,
        count them, that we know commit suicide,
the band wagon is full of corpses. The Congress votes for more
        overkill. Whatever bird outside my window
singing its tune for a moment resurrects the Sun and brings clarity
        to my memory, let him have our
        Praise and Progress,
and let the common bond which makes millennium song have our
        devoted following.

DARKNESS AND VASTNESS OF SPACE

At the end of the day
When I am tired sitting alone in my studio
        I often hear a train
sounding off in the distance, I never see the
        train, don't know what it contains,
it's dark and I feel sleepy, it is like a series of my poems
        unknown by many people; it is
        going to its destination.

THE MOVING MIND

I do not think it's in the skull
or merely in the toes, it may be
partly in the universe and everywhere
        it goes.

Mostly Spring and Summer

IMMEDIACY

Bound to the wind
like a bird to brightness
like a poem to inspiration
like a Musician to the Muse
like fire to the Sun
like motion to wind,
He, bound to the North Wind
        and all the learnings of its directions,
He, bound to the South Wind
        and all the learnings of its directions,
He, bound to the East Wind
        and all the mysteries of its orientation,
He, bound to the West Wind
        like Shelley in pursuit of the fire of the self,
he, along with you,
        surcharged follower,
        Sir Galaxy or Daisy Miller,
        sunflower or blossoming bridge,
he, along with you
        and the Sacred Elements
        were making a go of It
        and establishing a
        Wild Place of Now.

I BEGIN TO FIND FREEDOM

Masters who have been mastered—out there in
        the blizzard
of the 1st snow excited as boys about to have a
        fling, about
to slide, ride on their sleds for dear
        life, for
love of curves, cadenzas, breasts and hot
        chocolate;
going down, going up; Virgil in the underworld,
        Joyce in
the underpants, Molly blossoming; Masters
        who are
as calm as it is possible to be calm in the

                caves of
Datong, Dazu; Composers who have been composed
            by the
music from God knows where that you catch on to,
            that you
take note of; notes that have sounds coming from the
            stars; from
the most distant compelling curling soft lapping waves;
            I address
you all as I undress listening to your music, Bizet
            Bach,
Flamenco, Fauré, Debussy, Ravel, Vivaldi, nameless
            and
honored ones! I am naked and as exclamatory as I
            can be,
I begin the dance of the whirling dervish, I begin
            to obey.

FEBRUARY PRIVATE ACTIVITY

    Delicate
    still receptive thin uprisen
    branches of a young tree with its
            tinier
    tributaries extended, all, months
            before Spring,
    receiving the light of the sun, a quiet
            life inside,
    like Clarissas within their cells, and
            preparing
    as in prayer for what do you call them,
            green and waiting,
            leaves or songs?

THE REFLECTIONS OF THE LEAVES SHAKE ON
MY EARLY MORNING DESK; JUNE IN MAINE

That's
what I call
rapport—leaf and breeze—as a matter of
        air and Spring,
caress and shaking, early morning light and shade, I see
        them slightly
shaking, easy nicely does it, gently; but like
        you and me
breeze has its moods, its different movements, transformations,
        and for the
drenching past few days of coldness, dampness, greyness, and
        rain and rain
it was a stormy wind. The large new maple leaves
        however at this
moment radiant as can be were able to take it, to let
        it slide, I abide
by you said that which arranges long time unity. Dear
        twittering of abundant
many delicate large moving responsive leaves you taught
        Walt Whitman and
        many other lovers.

IT'S IN THE DARKENING AND
ENLIGHTENING WORKS

The mountains of snow are beginning to shrink,
        but
so am I; Spring is eventually slowly coming
        but what
about me, how far will I spring, leap
        sprint, run
without slipping ? another little snooze and
        then we do
a dance. Who's we ? You, all future people, all
        future galaxies.

WILDNESS-AND-MILDNESS

The practices of the wind often
          make me
wordy and then words shake like
          leaves
of a tree alone or of a whole dense
          forest even
Brazilian of leaves; sometimes make
          me seem
quite calm as in an undiscursive utter
          satisfaction;
whatever its necessities, unique and light,
          strong or
caressing, rampaging or at rest, I need
          it for
inspiration; respiration—so interdependent
          that yin and
yang whirl around at all different speeds
          seen and unseen.

HIGH BURST

If all
my bones
are put
into a cage
and they sing
like canaries—
if all
my bones
are put
into a cage
and they sing
like tall kings
if all my bones
are burning like
some golden birds
near the fire
of your eyes then
count me in and

then begin the
Ballad of the
Summoning sigh.

PRAYER, ACTIVE COMPANION IN PRIVACY

Just as there are
      streams in distant mountains
      it seems for a time unseen unheard
      there is the persistency and fluency of consciousness
      though sometimes everything seems vast, grey, very quiet,
then there is experienced motion making sound, the hidden or revealed
stream in its course, dance like, quick, curving, now and then revealing
its reflections of the sunlight or other relationships with rocks, skies,
leaves; rapid or slow, quiet or sparkling; and consciousness
      with all of its mythologies and metaphors,
      its relationship to clouds and
      necessity, spirit instructing
      the body in winding
      and worship.

APRIL 1

when april fool
arrived
      like a rabbit
      the calendar
      shook like the
      prophecy of a tree
      a green bird sang,
      like a poet flying
      and the shower
      expected was just
      on rhyme; time
      is the place for love
      and timelessness is
      what we do with it.

PROPHECY

Mourning dove
and my heart beat
you're carrying on some sort of duet,
it's April Fool's day and there's greyness and snow,
        you make your noises
        and I make mine,
there's a rhythm to it, a repetition slightly
        different every time,
at times we disappear, take flight, are only heard
        by those with the ears
of infinity; rain is predicted; Spring also you and I
        predict; the unseen Sun
and early morning and doves everywhere and purple finches
        and we are carrying on some
        sort of universal song.

ONE LIFE ANSWERS ANOTHER LIFE

You bring the sky
very close to me and then the source of
        all songs,
huge and noisy bluejay by my window,
        insistent
seeker and symbolist now suddenly flown into
        the nearby growing
pine tree, coolest autumn day, you let out
        any sort of piercing
sound; we receive each other's messages though
        Who knows What they mean
cannot be said; that's good luck I say; who wants
        to carry Concluded Meanings
        on his wings !find
your food, find your mate, as you fly you are inventing
        and finding your sky; the
heart beats faster; you are in the far distance now but I hear
        your cry like a remembrance.

PRECOCIOUS RECIPROCITY

Worms, you must be having a lot of thoughts and journeys
      these days with all this rain;
Robins, you must be having a lot of thoughts and hopping and
      research, there is hunger and drizzle;
students, it's near exam time so you must be ruminating
      and finally doing some reading;
lovers, you must be cozy thankful responsive touching upon
      the erotic zones of the world
(everywhere that is) in order to reaffirm and continue communications.

SUBSCRIBING TO BRILLIANCE

Now the dandelions are conquering the world,
these are the military conquests that I like,
thousands of them like Asian kings or lions or suns
      in the wide field;
you close your eyes and their military might multiplies;
      in life and death
let us memorize their magnificence.

RELATED TO THE NUMINOUS NOMENCLATURES

Gorgeous hawk,
I see you there in the dictionary,
between haw-haw and hawksbill turtle,
imagine what you are like in actuality and in Original Reality !
in flight or in huddled waiting, in thought and in gorgeous death or
      diving !
I can imagine some of your particular spots, beauty and motion,
      your daring,
your dangerous co-existence with us and storms and all kinds of
      weather, and other
birds and words of many feathers; here you are in the dictionary
      and it's not complete and
more words in distant futures will be added to it, here you

are surrounded by
thousands of words and many are in the memories of millions of
people everywhere and
will be in the writings that take wing, will be in the
barbarous and cultivated minds
of all sorts of astonished
strong ones in the future.

THE LUNATIC, THE LOVER, AND THE POET, AND THE COMMON READER

Common marvelous loons
are becoming scarcer in New Hampshire and elsewhere as
polluting destructive
unknowing lunatics commonplace as those who do not
love fully
are becoming like automobile exhaust more prevalent.
Prevent, prevent
destruction of this egg, this God; the Hairy Woodpecker,
the Blackpoll Warbler;
protect protect, angels and these birds; protect, protect
Milton, Whitman,
Marianne Moore, and these other relatives, that thousands of
generations have
served to color and make active; I sing also of you and
others in danger.

ORIENTATION

If I'm going to be around
and since it's human for what that's worth
to be reflective
I'd like some of my poems to learn from lakes
and their motions and
changing light in all seasons and from the
11th century Mi Fei;
his ideal in landscape painting was *ping dan,*

"calm, unassertive, without
emphasis or eccentricity."

*

little morning lake
quieted by clouds and mist,
reflective, thoughts like tiny ripples on
the tunic of the meditating Buddha, contained by
green wet mountains like some grey jewel, changing
light within the greyness to help philosophers grow,
you are, we are, buddhas as breathless in expectations,
        more books of thoughts,
        more necessary buddhas.

WONDER IS A SIGN THAT YOU HAVE WON

Is that just a robin
        or is it Magellan or
        some other fulfilled fulfilling
        colored captain of need, destiny,
        slightly wet determination ? anyway
        magnificence, this morning of haze
        and drizzle, suddenly in the apple tree,
        the small wide mature leaf laden
        tree also another magnificence for us to see;
        if you seek a purpose the way he seeks
        a worm and a future—be assured
        that one is—to wonder.

*

Decipher
if you can

the wishes of a waterfly
a polliwog, the nonsense songs of a
		wag
in a Shakespeare Play, Autolycus, O tell us
		more,
shimmerings of light in a drop of water on a leaf
		above a
dragonfly's wings, more lights as seen by the eyes
		of insects
or by the likes of galaxies of utterances, expressions of
		sentiments
so lyrical as to baffle Verdi and all all all philosophers

IT TAKES TIME FOR THE FAMILY
TO BEGIN TO MEET IN ETERNITY

Visitor
walking by all the islands of the world
		you levitate
for a while walking in air with the
		air of one
who has seen flowers and gods, one who has
		sensed lightness,
one who has had reverence for light, pebbles,
		shrubs, darkness,
listened to bird songs that have instructed dancers.
		When you visit
with reverence a gift, any gift, person, mountain,
		stream, poem
you remember so well so pleased you are its cousin.

ABUNDANT RELEASE OF POEMS

All these years
I have let myself go
where I have gone those who have to know
		will know.

INSISTENCE IS SO COSMIC

Who am I keeping company with this morning ?

mosquitoes, grass, daisies, the breeze, a lake,
     and as always more or less my imagination
the sound now of wind through the leaves,
     slight, and before I heard my necessity say
     write and before I seemed to hear my
     talking to my Self (which includes
     you and all these things, sticks,
     insects, trees of all ages)
the various unknown birds, before my Words—
     and after them ? let that thought float
     like the quick breeze over
     the lake; I'm all alone
up here, if you exclude the blades of grass,
     the whippoorwills, the cicadas, the slight
     sounds of water
by the shore and you and God and all that goes
     with this
and my book of poems by Wm. Carlos Williams;
     what's honking ? some present
     themselves insistently in green
     and some in print.

NEIGHBORS IN THE PURE REALM

Poem, what a snake you must be,
     your whole body listens close to the ground;
poem, what a bird you must be,
     your whole song listens close to the sky;
man, what a poem you must be,
     your whole universe speaks close to the gods.

Now that I am an owl you will find me useful,
now that I am an owl you will find yourself wise,
now that I am a bear you will find me
        heavy elemental,
if war is necessary we will bleed; before
        necessity or insanity
        makes us die
let us stomp, make music, present a
        pageant.
Now that we are extremely lost and lonely let us
        talk to all things as
        our required brothers.

A PARTIAL ACCOUNT FOR PRACTICALITY, PLEASURE, PROCREATION

We need to get what we need
and what we imagine we need we sometimes
need too
said the entire body and the imagination to the
heightened giraffe
who ate in its elegant lofty way
the highest leaves;
the elegant spotted long legs were helpful, it
could run 31 mph,
the elegant long neck (6 1/2 ft. long) can make it
tower above the
others in the wide restaurant of life; the prehensile
grasping tongue
(sometimes 20 inches long) is practical; when need be
that serviceable tongue
can also precisely clean the giraffe's fine nose and ears.
Necessity helped it
superbly rise to
the Occasion.

WHAT CYMBALS AND SYMBOLS DO SHAKE ?

What vines do you eat,
        caterpillar
become poet, one who desires to be
        divine ?
what wine do you drink, Dionysus,
        that you
make us dance with the vines tickling
        our nakedness
as we clap our hands to make time pass ?
        what songs
do you sing, Orpheus, to make us follow
        with caterpillar,
unicorn, animals born of the sacred being,
        angels consistently
following ? the soul of the hand, the soul of
        the foot,
vibrations related to all blood flowing sources,
        what do you
touch, what do you reach, what do you teach
        as the dancers
swoon ? soon the music increases its tempo and
        the whirling brides
and husbands of darkness and light, of vines and
        the seas, bring
to the festival the stirrings that urge all to break
        into Spring.

REDBREASTS AND PANOPLY APLENTY

A host of robins, better than
        bishops, returning
and well-fed it seems and large enough
        to fill the coming
Spring universe with religious needs somewhat
        satisfied, songs
and families of future songs, *suddenly*
        this company *arrived*
shaking the tiny branches of the ample pine
        trees outside my window.

There is still snow and there is much greyness
and so these well feathereed
sometimes flighty constituents of good hope
give color to our Moment.

CAPABLE OF DESIRE AND CONTINUITY

How busy
the balmy woodpecker is
like a business man at his computer
only generally better looking, more alert,
more nimble, feathery, quickly capable of
flight, all of us with a sense of danger,
all of us hungry, busy busy with worries
and looking for food, for ourselves and
sometimes for others.

WELL SUPPLIED WITH FANCIES AND DESIRES

Yawning
loudly at the beginning of Spring
in Maine on a late Sunday afternoon as the snow is
melting
he fancies himself a lion, and forthwith becomes a lion,
he ventures forth
into the kitchen as a proud mature lion covered with the gold
of experience, and
having read poetry he ventures out up and down streets by trees
that will soon have
some blossoms and he feels that his sniffing is evocative,
that when he yawns again
some lioness will show her golden belly. He just slightly
shakes his mane and swaggers
slowly as he walks uphill.

EXOTIC THOUGHTS IN VACATIONLAND

So many yawns like so many lions,
    it was a hot summer day and the reader lay there or sat there
        or slouched there almost naked
reading a variety of books, I'll spare you the scattered list;
        in Kenya the wind blew the tall tall grass
        and gorgeous slouchy lions, not all
        so young, snarled, rolled over
        had the wind tickle their ears,
imitated the writer.

WM. JAMES SAID THE MILLENNIUM WOULD NOT COME AS LONG AS A SINGLE COCKROACH SUFFERED FROM UNREQUITED LOVE

O single cockroach, what is God planning for you ?
        what's in the Works ? what's in
        the plumbing ?
Mermaid and Merman, have you plummeted to the
        depths of the sea
finding the original eggs, the original tests ? swishing
        your tails
you ascend the wave's unfurling like a flower in
        the wind;
but let's return to our brother cockroach, Walt
        Whitman
wishes to help him out, St. Francis wishes to help him out,
        Allen on the go
in the collected works wishes to help him out; go and
        live with the animus,
the anima, even C. G. Jung needs a push; "O I think
        I could turn
and live with the animals"; go enter the alleys
        of need, the
highways of the undescribable heaven; ring the marriage
        bells, bring the
students, the young lovers in need upward, touching
        whispering, fingering, finding,
        upward to the very
        cheek of God.

I always knew I was
related to birds in migration

it's how come we're here   all of us
and sometimes we sing   and sometimes we fly

I always knew I was
related to fish   smell

it's even better than the Encyclopedia Brittanica
for getting procreation   recreation

kippers   you say
keep it   I say
hold it   I pray
swallow   I say

the sea has many fish dreams
I always knew we were seals plunging
into the water   pursuing each other

slippery   quick   pleased with our selves
and each other   pursuing each other

THERE WAS ALSO THE SUN,
THERE WERE MILLIONS OF FISH,
THERE WERE A FEW PHOTOGRAPHERS

I saw rabbits
in the Arctic   many of them   many of them

running running   they were perfect
they were angelic

not far away

white whales   white whales

many of them   many of them

singing singing   teaching their children

the alphabet   the musical scale

navigational mysteries

bibles spouting

I saw white birds   white birds
thousands of them   the splurging of the sea
the rolling and tossing and speed of those graceful waves
the leaping of those thousands of rabbits

and your poems wanted to keep them company

"MEN WORK TOGETHER, I TOLD HIM FROM THE HEART, / WHETHER THEY WORK TOGETHER OR APART." ROBERT FROST

Look
at an object
sky, sea, tree,
flower, river, any person,
we are looking at a subject, we are its object,
we take sustenance from it; even when we are asleep
it is taking sustenance from us; the sea imitates a flower; a sky imitates
you; the tree imitates a second; the hour
imitates you; the river imitates a sentence; you imitate the
    the beginning of these singing
    companions, similes always
    are suggesting that you visit
    a relative for this particular holiday.
A hermit relative says
    in some instances
    as between words
(as between awakenings we need sleep)
    we like space; so
    stay where you are,
and sing of me in Walden hidden;
    of the Apsarases in the
    river of milk in the
    sky humming. A
humming bird approaches a tree.

SENTENCES AND SENSIBILITY

What is it about a glance that throws us at a
      chance moment
into something like an erotic dance or
      prelude to it?
a young so called student looks at me
      and my fantasies
take me to Tahiti, I learn of beauty in
      sonnets by looking
at her form, her youthful glow makes me
      go wherever romance
ever went. The eyes, the eyes, have it, the
      glances of the dancers
put us into balmy whirlwinds of thoughts. We
      read a story together
to gather eventually understanding of love for
      communication, for some sort
      of temporary charged
      sense of unity.

THE LINES CHANGE, DARKEN AND BRIGHTEN

I'd rather be read than dead,
rather be all colors too, the rainbow
      in its
coming and going, the butterfly in its
      metaphysics
and in its particular flowers. I am ready
      for you to read me
to need me, to see you is to please me; peruse
      the literature
thoroughly, purr, meow on the grand scale or mountain;
      we are tigers.

TIME IS OR SEEMS CONTROLLED THOUGH THERE IS BOTH HERACLETIAN FIRE AND CERTAINTY BEYOND OUR REFLECTIONS

The tiniest chickadee
        hops in the tall forest of the asparagus ferns
        a buddhist bamboo grove in miniature;
        everybody's body a thought, a bud, and so
we grow rooted in the moving earth, or moving in the
        changing music of the sky; it seems the width of
        stillness, central summer now, summit
        of a garden's fulfillment; but nothing is
still, an atom moves along with the planetary motions
        and the birds not so far from our bare feet.
        Heat is vast and yet here in the shadows
        these thoughts are cool and
        satisfied enough.

THE PLANET AS THE TEMPLE'S INNER SHRINE

I imagine something similar to it
        is going on in all of nature
        rocks, fish, weeds, rabbits
        and so on,
all night a varied noisy downpour of Spring rain and
        the earth seeming passive
        as it takes, as it learns,
        seeping it in,
this constant more or less consciousness I mean—
        in *everything*—bird, flower,
        worm, the delicate
        accompanist
outside my window trilling his few notes, in search of a mate,
        in search of a universe,
        continuity;
even in sleep dreams, like myths in seeds, fables
        in forests, this more or less
        continuous
vibration of thought in whales, in whippoorwills, in crickets,
        in the single weed or monk,
        alone, alone,

and yet all this chorus, this bathed swaying of prayers,
continuous, unfathomable,
something like song.

SECLUDED ECSTASIES

The darning needle
over the stream, the yogi by the River,
the acrobat on the water

whatever miracles you perform
are very visible to the miraculous beings
who make the true musical scores

flickering of light
under the wings of the darning needle
above the mind of the hermit.

THOUGH IT'S HAPPENED BEFORE IT IS AS NEW
AS THE FIRST PROMULGATION OF STARS

One gets pent up
like a raccoon under a lot of logs?
like a saint glum, uninspired?
like larva almost motionless?
like a fearful-tired-depressed person?
until again I become better than Lewis and Clark and explore
rivers, northwest territories,
like promulgating Zeus out on the universe of the town,
I finger your figure,
thighs, knees, tits, toes, nose, ears, backside, and back again to
curves under the breast,
it's happened since the beginning when sex became timely and
so I slip and move back and forth
consciously unconsciously
preceeding Jung and forever after and somewhat satisfied and squirm
and spill and spell
the way raindrops do upon the fields, your body of beauty

moves a little, moist,
rabbits perk up their ears, *putti* content say we've seen this
happen before.

INDENTURED AMENITIES

Meadows
and mellowness and unheard and slightly
      heard
melodies after love making, and dew and
      new
Spring flowers, fields and fields, undulating
      fields
of them, flourishing of vague memories,
      centuries
of them wherever there is need, seeds, songs,
      tenderness.
Sheep nibbling, goats lifting their heads, shaking
      their ears,
cows in the mist sisters to clouds, geniuses of
      paradise.

THE BEGINNING OF AN EMBRACE

The waves
long long vista of them
rising up inevitable curving over foam
      and sun
sparkle that the combined force of gods and goddesses
      cannot rival
waves accompanied by their unprescribable sound
      rise to the
occasion of the vast dim blue sky, centuries
      of moon and
movement and earth's thoughts preparations the
      inevitable
cadence of this liquid opera, the combined power
      of all poems

cannot equal its soft and strong sumptuousness
              and surprise.

SPECIFYING THE LIQUIDS OF PROCREATION

Again a night
amidst the legs of the darkness
the phosphorescent glow the wavering sea anemone
              the murmurings
of small waves, grottoes of barnacles and sea weed, instructors
              of musicians
who come up for air; nibblings nibblings nibblings in the
              meantime
send sea horses dancing like upgoing snowflakes in the
              wind, currents
of wavering streams wetness visited by purple and orange
              and other colored
masqueraders, fertility's festival, millions of
              years in
cooperation with the billowing sea; astronauts of the deep
       '   sputter their stars.

WAVERING UNACCOUNTABLE VICTORIES

Gasp, grasp, civilization is making summarizing summer
              on winter nights
possible, so the body-and-mind in a dance or trance re-enact
              creation, coming
together, falling apart, returning sleepy and waking in intercourse
              the waves of course
have an urgent way of their own, we bounce, we drift,
              we drowse, we douse, we doze,
we chose to play as dolphins do, don't forget to
              sleep or slide into
the unseen prominence; such politics is only for the
              victorious.

EXTENSIONS OF CO-OPERATION

Backside of a horse in its barn,
  some darkness,
smell of hay, some flies, a ladder
  to the loft,
memories of childhood in Cantù, mine;
  leaping
into the haystack, a mystic moment when
  I felt the
cow's udders, pulled the soft heavenly
  things; we
look upon the world, the sky, the well-formed
  rump of stallion,
the mottled geography of the largesse of cow
  as nourishment.

BARNS AS TEMPORARY FINE SMELLING TEMPLES

Mountainous backsides of moon bellied cows, looming large
  as the mother
of the earth, mothers more likely and where the deuce are
  the roaming
fathers ? don't give me any of that bull, they said
  after a while;
but these magnificent cows kept munching and occasionally
  mooed,
occasionally moved, breezes and mosquitos, the great
  smell of
grass, clover, Queen Anne's lace; in daylight calm,
  queen like,
in darkness and barns they loomed large, munched, moved,
  and occasionally mooed.

CHILDREN OF ADAM AND EVE,
HIGH GRASS, AUGUST

Mowing like rowing
               waves of green
               numerous numerous
               bees buzz around us
like light, the grass collapses, sways, perks up,
               the whiff of wonder, the
               smell of new cut grass,
the feel of long grass on our bare feet, the erotic
               zones awaken, the elves
in imagination are active, the noisy lawn mower
               and erogenous zones
are buzzing; responsive I push and pull, uphill,
               downhill, sweating
profusely, dripping, dripping, pleasure makes us shiny;
               mounds, bumps, weeds, bugs,
tangles, temptations, joy and the shaking head, it's as if
               music were pushing and propelling us.

PEASANT PLEASANT WORK

Raking Raking Raking, Making the Rake's Progress,
               Sweating
Sweetheart, I picture it, I do it, bending over,
               picking up grass,
smelling it, finding it, feeling it, warm, it's
               agriculture at its
best; believe me the earth has memories, has
               messages, vibrations
get to us, we sweat, sweetheart, we strip somewhat
               for summer work.
You say go to it, work at it, mow, mosey, relax
               and then return to
               Raking Raking.

GOOD LUCK HERE MEANS SOME KIND
OF ACTIVE AMOROUSNESS

Between the arm pit and the breast . . . . . am I becoming
                              a specialist ?
no, no, familiar, nosey, sort of floating, but pretty much as
                              foolish as ever,
no technician or computer—instead imagist of
                              Me and Mystery,
                              Mickey and Minnie Mouse,
                              Centaur and Maiden,
                              Antony and Cleopatra,
imaginative as well as biological with
                              amorous luck;
                              there are places
on her body that I prefer to favorite Cities or Gardens;
there is her complete body which includes our souls;
I am astronomically and intuitively related to that which I prefer
to textbooks of Geography, Science, or Theology;
                              warm knowledge
                              under the cupola
                              of that little breast
                              is often best.

THE MEANING OF THE BODY

It is not geography,
it is not oceanography,
it is not sky—
though at times it
seems to have come from there,
it cannot be photographed,
even though it is known
by seeing, by touching,
by desiring and desiring,
known nearer than
your own identity,
the sounds in a sea shell
seem to echo it

All night long the sports of sex horsed around, centaurs, sent
      their sperm into the tides of the thighs,
or thighs of tides, cavorted, haunches rose, thick rhythms
      in the night accompanied by transistor music
splurged, lounged, she revealed her giardino rather pubblico,
      he at 1st like a stout and hairy cub ate at
      the jar of honey, then sure enough like
      17 fountains he displayed, or like centaurs
      in foam he played; the static shot at
      all their pores like little arrows;
      the hot jazz poured over them
      like black strap molasses, it
      was good for the health.

THE LUMINOUS JOY WHICH GIVES VIBRANCE TO THE BODY'S TONE: TUNE FROM THE BRIGHT SKY

O health, O flourishing opulence which supports the
      world, which procreates the gods and
      children, and gives songs
      to all that flames
      in green,
why are there so few poems to you ? When we become sick so as
      to become self-conscious, of this cough,
      this tumor, this tomb, this
      constant bleeding or loss
      of breath, this
stunning thought of death, then fear and feebleness interrupt
      the rhythm, the river goes dry,
      and Gerontion is at the
      window sill.
Dust has its dusty element of truth. But "one element
      doth not a universe make."
The opulent lovers instead, their naked feet in glory and
      in dew,
spread their wild wings. Whatever ecstasies we have they are
      reflections of that flight,
      that Light.

AFTER MATH OR FIGURING THINGS OUT

And after many times
of making love or having been made by it
or being where we were in on the making of music
or being in giddiness and memory we were again and again
          where the beginning of freedom
          is known

then in the dark

as if ascending the two of us
          as if the sky were sea
          as if the stars were flowers

as if we had in delirious drunkenness and urgings
gathering the treasures of the sea, the sea tastes,

suddenly
after hours of drifting   lifting legends in our arms
of ascent descent   assent   swooning
giving lessons in smiling and sleeping to the archaic

gods, goddesses, sea urchins, sea weed, sea music, balminess,

drifting   floating   high again   splurging   kissing again
          almost fainting again

in a new freedom in darkness talking for hours

WHAT THE RUFFLED SHAMAN TOLD
MIRCEA ELIADE ". . . SHE HAS BEEN COMING
TO ME EVER SINCE, AND I SLEEP WITH HER
AS WITH MY OWN WIFE . . . SOMETIMES SHE
COMES AS A WINGED TIGER, I MOUNT IT
AND SHE TAKES ME TO SHOW ME DIFFERENT
COUNTRIES." *SHAMANISM* (PP. 72-73)

Can you pull yourself up just a little bit more ? and
          those wings that are like flames
          can you make them change into

water occasionally ? a public park
is better with fountains; now that we're both wet and
        reading the scriptures the hotel bed keeps
        growling and dropping golden coins into
        purses which we can transform into our
        currency as we sleep and the walls keep
        pushing us around; the walls occasionally
become different rivers that have relatives swimming in them
        who teach us tricks they learned in
        different countries.

She has been coming to me ever since; I everlastingly know
        she makes me and my wife growl better.

A SELECTION OF BRIEF MESSAGES FROM
A RADIO TELESCOPE SPECIALIST

I will tell you a few things that
        I love about the universe,
        galaxies keep on changing all the time,
        the whole system such as you and I
        keeps on changing, some stars are
very young, some very bright like you, some
        dancers burn themselves up,
        a few billion years, very
        recently; many galaxies
are spinning around; I observe and I interpret light waves,
        I listen and listen to Debussy,
        Sappho and others; listen
and observe; now we can walk on the Moon,
        stars like to form in groups,
        look at the Seven Sisters for
Instance; the scattered light comes out as
        blue; therefore the sky is a
        Blue Angel diffuse;
        lying in the field of grace
        in the southern hemisphere
you can see especially well clearly the
        Milky Way; celestial cows
        seduced by Zeus
all together scatter light waves; our
        weather and oceans and moods

and myths must all be
related to this, and hot stars, and young sisters
and Dionysus in ecstasy
in the Nebulae.
At the Moment it's
putting forth a strong Spiral.
"We really are the children of stars" which is more
than an interesting thought.

CHANGES IN THE ATMOSPHERE

What do we know
about dinosaurs
or family squabbles ?
footprints of dinosaurs give us maps to study as those of
fleas or sandpipers;
I think of our prayers as sandpipers; people often seem to
have a hard time
getting along together; the kiss of a genuine thought opens
the rock,
from it comes water. Niagara Falls is an infinitisimal
second in
the Bhagavad-Gita. I sneeze and deserts move. The
rattlesnake
searches for food and the future. We are beggars on the desert;
if our
entire lives look at the land, sky, stone, any creature,
each other
with undefinable genuine love our flighty attempts at
definitions
like the shadows of startled sandpipers make a temporary
pattern that we can
also celebrate.

THOUGH YOU WERE EXPECTING IT
YOU WERE SURPRISED

Suppose
that short plump dark haired woman
        in the train station
is an opera singer and the hunched over sturdy
        black adolescent
is also one and that the thin woman with glasses
        who might be a
middle aged school teacher is one of the world's great
        sopranos it's
very possible and suppose the burly guy with a
        plaid shirt
and the red baseball cap is a wacky basso and
        suppose the
three short Sicilian women who meet and exclaim in
        their dialect
could carry on like song birds in olive trees or
        shout with delight,
certainly all of this is more than possible since
        everyone is a buddha
and all men and women Whitman says are poets and all
        of God's children got rhythm,
suppose they at the moment read your mind as if it
        were a musical score and
        Obeying your Impulse
        All Together began
        to Sing!

FAIRFIELD BEACH

        The child
        by the sea makes designs and I
                watching
        admiring make designs and what
                has designed
        the sea ripples and the waves of the white
                frequently
        flying many sea gulls and the timeliness of
                the tides

330

and the curves of the high grass and the drifting
    of the
sail boats, some white and green sails, some with the
    orange and yellow
and red sails, what has designed the imagination and the
    need of
the child with her crayon in her hand satisfies
    beyond my tenure.

PLATO TOO, AS IF DESCENDING IN A PARACHUTE

Parents
too
are
about
to
be
born
when
the
daughter
is
pregnant
grandparents
too
and
Krishna
and
crowd
and
all
the
tribes
and
Adam and Eve
when
a
child
is
born

331

TO HELP FIND THE WAY HELP FIND THE
INTIMATIONS OF IMMORTALITY

It's in ways
a divine comedy,
that means making life-making choices
  that amount to
hell, purgatory, or heaven; what guides are
  attracted to you,
which do you keep in heart, like Virgil and
  Beatrice, *etc.*
Dante was practical making choices for his tradition
  and individual talent;
he fainted several times; he slept, he dreamt,
  he begged, he prayed,
he listened to prayers, he said to hell with you
  to intimate distractions,
possible deals, destructions; he was Florentine precise,
  mathematical and in love
with the music of the spheres, St. Thomas, St. Francis,
  St. Bernard as was
possible given the length of his nose, the limitations
  of everyman's knowledge;
but return to salvation which is ineffable personal,
  we make our choices,
plan as best we can (realizing that health, weather,
  friends, dangers, and the
cosmos influence) our travel schedules; how many cities, days,
  cantos ? we say to the
saints and ancestors of our individual "élan vital" keep it
  going, continue to show
  somehow your awe,
  your respect for
  the divine.

BEFORE THE DAZZLING DAYS OF MANY
COLORFUL FESTIVALS

Now
do you feel noble enough
completely satisfied enough this late vast

sunny very cool
September Maine afternoon with all the trees
        still sumptuous,
generous, at ease in a slight breeze, knowing
        that they have been
your brothers, your sisters, all along, that
        what their tributaries
and intelligent roots know accompanies
        your knowledge in an
indivisible way ? you have many moods and you're
        awfully serious about them
sometimes; and they are also responsive to weather,
        seasons, histories,
complex for scientists; you're on the same planet earth
        this gorgeous day
before the days when they will shed their leaves
        the way a Mother
sheds her tears over the body of Christ, they will
        shed their leaves
the way calendars for centuries have shed their days;
        so much is giving itself away;
it looks very generous like a guru with non-possessive love
        who is abundantly comic
        beyond all comprehension.

JUST RETURNED TO A SECLUDED SPOT
NEAR A SMALL HILL I AM SATISFIED

Now,
exactly moon struck now, here, on a slanted
        uphill secluded
street in Maine, how can something so far away and illuminated
        by a power
energy still more distant enlarge my love of here and everywhere
        so much?
it does; I see it, on this very cool getting dark Spring night as
        days will begin
to get warmer, see it like a halo, clear, for the energies of your
        best thoughts,
see it so that my love for this spot this moment has emanations
        is patriotic,
see it, small round perfect light Moon, between the thin branches

333

of a tree
that now has tiny leaves. While walking in the lesser dark a
      half hour ago
I saw the many quiet soft flames uprisen large, buddhas, buds of
      a wide delicate enlightening
      magnolia tree.

PREDESTINED INSTRUCTIVE BROTHER

The sentence
like the motion of a fine long snake
      with changing
colors of flames of blue and green knows
      when to pause,
listen with its whole body and its relationship
      to its subtle need,
knows when to raise its enigmatic emblematic
      kinglike head
and look in upraised stillness like an ancient
      priest; it's time
to move on ancestral instincts say, commandments
      long before Moses
make it slither between the tall soft grasses; familiar
      with the earth, the
sun, the seasons, prehistoric insects, and to be
      discovered paths, it
      knows when to stop.

THE CONTINUING DAY AFTER A BIRTHDAY

Aren't those songs, bird songs, poems,
aren't those active self-green-confident fulfilled many
      summer leaves
making you expansive outgoing ready to shake if there's
      a breeze
ready to sound human if there's a Keats or a Marvell?
      Marvel
at this or that and you put on spirit expand saunter

like summer
air light, linger like fragrances in the doused evening,
    smells of magnolia,
what's magnificent becomes you as you enter the
    field of intuitions.

AND THE DEW THAT COOLED OUR HANDS

Smelling the inside of each pea pod
    cool fresh
I enter the green cathedral, I can
    remember
rain and sustain the wide leaves of
    plants and
I become green myself, a vine of many
    emblems.
We become what we were in Eden before the
    inventions
of fathers. We remember the 1st rains that came
    to our bodies.

FLOWERS BEING RECORDED IN HER NOTEBOOK
WHILE I AM SLIGHTLY DOZING

Summer heat
and everybody who is awake is half asleep
    and nimbuses
around sheep grow thicker, a sound of a
    helicopter, a
sound of a bee, the sounds of children playing
    in the distance;
the abundance of pine trees, oak trees,
    different shades of green
all still, the distant vague sound of a
    lawnmower, the very
very nearby sounds of my thoughts; Grace in
    her studio sits painting.

It was raining so
then there was the king and queen,
I mean the seer and the magnolia tree seen,
      bush all of buds full
and wet by the slight and pervasive and vast drizzle;
      dizzy with desire to see and be the seer
      I walked not in a hurry by it;
a reign and communion which insures the public power;
      wet we take ourselves to whatever it is
      growing and say to each other
we knew each other, we have insisted on this meeting,
      also poem and reader
      have been insistent.

THAT WHICH IS RELATED TO FAITH, HOPE, AND CHARITY

When
I think of how the different colors
      of vegetables
absolutely please me I get religious,
      I think
we're meant for each other, Cézanne
      for the colors
of his victorious mountain; the humming bird
      for the colors of
the mouth of its flower; the pageant of the purple
      of the eggplant;
the radiance of the red of the tomatoes, the radiance
      of the delicate
pale yellow glow of the slender squash, the freckled
      freshness of the
zucchini green just handed to me; I know there
      are attractions
that have been in the nourishing process; I know
      that Mary
wanted a child and so the Annunciation was born,
      I know that the
Sun has much to do with the rainbow, that the red

cupola of Santa Maria
del Fiore at the center of Florence attracts thoughts of
God; that vowels
have color, that benevolent beliefs color our
hopeful achievements.

A Light Long Branch

NO ONE CAN COUNT HOW OFTEN
WE CAN BE BORN

Getting close to a poem that you like
or getting close to a place that you love
      where you were once born
makes you beam, I've been there said the
      Muse and new
music occurs, it comes out of the stones, out
      of the syllables,
you get off the glowing and swaying boat and you
      walk around
for a while in say Genova and you become
      more generous,
you give the 1st reader you meet a kiss
      or a new poem.

AS FRESHMEN APPROACH THE AUTUMN CAMPUS

If necessary—if called for—if your need is pure enough—
      if you are ready—
any subject will do—will do what ? will do you . . .
      the exchange
will be like Odysseus meeting Athena, practical and magical.
      No stone
must be left unturned if we are to hear the songs of the
      radiant beginners.
A teacher, that is one who desires blossoming, one who desires
      dance and the exchange,
sees a new student who is an old poet, ancient with listening,
      ready for vibrations,
the novice takes a tentative step, writes a musical phrase in his
      notebook, the field flames.

There's a community of readers,
        hundreds
of people with noses pointed towards the center
        of their books,
it's been snowing for weeks, the 2nd big blizzard
        going on now;
and people are getting nearer to Montaigne and to books
        about mountains
and sex and food and politics; some are reading poems,
        hibernating in the
darkness of phrases, drowsing amidst sounds of the
        inner music;
outside the greyness and wind and drizzle persist;
        hundreds of people
by their reading lights in Maine are having fantasies and
        thoughts, are wanting to
        conquer the world
        with words.

ARISTOTLE: "GOD MOVES THE UNIVERSE
        BY BEING DESIRED."

    Now
    look at the object with
    desire so that it becomes radiant; is
        that the way
    the Sun looks at earth, at us, making
        plants grow,
    helping our souls light up so that we think
        of Juliet
    or bird or flower or god that we need,
        that we
    rejoice in ? O radiant universe, my
        waking
    wandering changing desired companion, these
        lights
    that we become and celebrate let them be
        helpful

342

gifts for children, lovers, wanderers in the
   future.

THE LOVER WATCHES THE PLANET

Not stopped by doors or walls the music proceeds and
   from a distance of nearby
enters my room, enters your soul, the sun enters
   the seed, the bridegroom
the magic house of love, the bird's song rides through
   the sunlit air, the leaves
like response or applause shake, more abundant than
   Shakespeare or Whitman,
the praise or prayer of the listener gives Prospero a future,
   the child or Miranda will admire
   you listening to a poem.

TAKING DIRECTIONS FROM WHAT'S
EVEN BETTER THAN BALANCHINE

Now and always the body language of the poem
      tells us much
as does the direction and business of the flight
      of the bee, the
body language of Nureyev dazzles as he leaps,
      the poem's
movement music informs us so as to at least
      momentarily
transform the soul; sound sense to make the
      soul; the belief
of the body language, its gestures, arouses sleeping
      beauty; while the
sleeper in the Self is very deep in that so called
      Other World which is
our eternity its dreams and images appear as
      they did to Miranda;
"Thou wast a cherubim didst save me"; O always

strange New World
that has such graceful saving choreography
in its Necessity.

INTROSPECTIVE ASTRONAUT

I wish to penetrate the flower of the flower
to sing the very
living light
to enter the dreams of all colors
to bring the very
living vibrations
to move within the Self where
all gods waiting
to be met
have music sessions, to celebrate the
Everywhere Within.

THE NOTES WEREN'T STARTED JUST TONIGHT
THOUGH THEY STARTLE NOW

It's dark out there
but how many poems are going to come in tonight
through the window?
the city's lights are lit up, the bridges lit up, the stars
started sending us
their messages long ago to reach me at this moment
as I look up
stirred up vaguely thinking of you, of what your little hand
did to me
and the rest of you, it doesn't allow me to calm down;
we pronounce
songs enough of desire in our waiting or sleep to enlighten
the lovers reading
these notes.

FOR ME THE TRAVELLING SUN KNEW
HIS PLACE IN RELATIONSHIP TO YOU

Who will remember those petals ?
they are gone, for 15 years the petals of the pear trees
    visited my window
blessed the air, made blossom background for pictures of
    our growing daughters,
gave messages to angels, spoke somehow to the Sun, new
    words returned each Spring
    to the two pear trees
and today while I was at work they were cut down . . .
    I say to my future poems and
    to my daughters' futures,
somehow remember them; God desiring beauty made
    them so strong and delicate
that Desdemona was their sister, the pear trees
    seen in different seasons,
blessed by snow or moonlight, whispered to by wind,
    did I thank you enough ?
Never complaining that I complained so much. There to greet
    me like the most modest poetry,
and now you are not there; I will greet you wherever I see
    you in future lives like angels.

CENNINO CENNINI IN HIS BOOK OF ADVICE
FOR PAINTERS: "FIRST KNEEL AND PRAY,
THEN PAINT; PAINT THE SKY
WITH 'LA POLVERE DI LAPIS LAZULI' . . . ."

    Ashes to sky,
    dust to eternity,

pray and the rainbow will come to you disguised as a follower of
Christ and will tell you—*now now make me visible*, O fabulist of
tempera and time, O source of innocence refreshment in your frescoes;
    what fire what burning worlds
    what comets with their tigers
    what bones of great great prophets
    of all our grand grand grand grandfathers
    what lizards and what lightnings

what luxuries of summer intensity
went into the memory of the phoenix
who is seen in the transformed changing
light of la polvere la povertà
la processione di lapis lazuli
first kneel and pray, say to the space where a moment ago an
 Angel was with all his fires all his poems all his
religions and rainbows   STAY   STAY
NOW   NOW   I   SEE   YOU

WARM PEACEFUL MAINE DAY, SLIGHT BREEZE

Bird
whose name I do not know
and who has already flown away
though I heard a moment ago your high brief
        incomparable song
your most precise clear undecipherable by me
        pure note,
I saw you on the familiar branch of the tree near
        my porch, my
perch, my search, our mutually needed presence,
        I saw your
plump whitish belly, you, delicate, rather long and fine,
        with the
practical necessity and amusing condition of long flickering tail; ·
        my notes
probably undecipherable to you say precisely that we were meant
        for each other.

BEGINNERS IN EROS' THEATER

The body language—of lips—
        relaxed—
or curved, twisted, tight from
        years of
cynicism—or alert grape like
        plump

perhaps even slightly purple ready to
      kiss, to
speak by pressing, to show whatever learning
      we are capable of
from various divinities of love, Hindu,
      Aegean, Ghanean,
go on, show your vocabulary silently
      exploring other lips,
all parts of the body; move them ever
      so slightly or bite
sharply-and-gently enough; we know when we
      receive instructions from
      the gods only the
      infinite is enough.

IN ALL WAYS KNOWN AND UNKNOWN
PROTECT THE COMMANDMENT

Now
what was I dreaming of
before I came into the world that made me later
      insist upon
so persistently so sumptuously mandala and cupola of
      Duomo—
Como, Roma, Firenze, Siena, Taj Mahal, Xanadu, on and on—
      all I know
is that what made me dream makes me dream still
      before the
first sounds, gestures, responses to the light, beginning of
      my arousing
pilgrimage, it was the message commandment that nourished me,
      saved me.

UNDERSTANDING THAT WE CANNOT NAME THE
HOLY SPIRIT WE REVERENCE EVERY VOICE

Voice,
    what a great mystery you are,

in ways like a flower but in child or man or
      woman more moving,
in that way like a galaxy great mystery, unique gift
      to every child, man, woman;
strange how I think everything has a voice, the tree,
      the star,
how I feel sure that whatever creates music has its
      messengers deep in the
fibers of everything, in all the feelings not only of the
      human race. To speak to you
lambs and lions and crickets and gazelles must have been
      speaking to Adam and Eve.

ACTIVE IN THE EARLY RENAISSANCE OR EMERSON: "THE EYE OF GENIUS IS CREATIVE."

How much have I eyed
I   I   I   I   ay   ay   ay
identified with, soul
of the object becoming
my I, how many
Nativity Scenes, now one
by Bernardo Daddi,
have I seen, have I
invented, how many
have seen me in need, in
changing forms of nativity ?

SERVING LIKE ANGELS AN UNWILFUL PURPOSE

Now what can we do with all
      these
beautiful paintings that I have
      returned to
for more than 50 years, seen, sort of
      forgotten ? forever
remembered ? why worry ? since what made
      the painter paint

has its strange way with the memory of the
    respectful visitor;
these scenes of Canaletto and Guardi now
    float back
into the mind like gondolas when benevolent
    associations are
    necessary.

JACOPONE DA TODI (OR MONET): "ORDINA QUEST' AMORE, O TU CHE M'AMI."

The 1st brush stroke,

now where will we go ?
what made me do it ? brush stroke, I look at you
    and you lead me on colorfully
    but it takes time though it will
    in its frame be still, the kind
    of stillness that will make
    thousands of tourists spell
    out their momentary being,
    that makes the Louvre shake;
having a dialogue with you, painting, as
you begin to show my Vision, as I look
another direction is given and in the spell
I touch you with more wet colors, Order
will be made like still music.

That makes the lover dance.

WE ARE NOTES AND LAUGHTER ON THE GREAT MUSICAL SCALE

Now making it again . . . what are you making ?. . .
    mountains of course and together
    we can move them . . .
love of course and together we can prove it . . .
    music of course and we hear

349

everybody noteworthy in it. Religion of course,
you've got a sense of humor.

BECOMING MORE NIMBLE AND
AMUSED AT MY NEW TASK

To protect the ripening tomatoes from frost,
I have a new task;
I've become alert and professional about it;
every night before supper
I go out there and quickly cover each tomato plant
upheld by its green stick,
its small and large tomatoes expanding in view,
cover each plant with a large
plastic bag, at times feel like
a French dressmaker tucking the skirts in,
feel very familiar with these
ladies, and as it grows dark
I feel sort of Rabelaisian
there bending over and
enjoying a whiff of
the odor from the
nearby marigold
bushes.

THE SEA OF RECREATION THAT FIRST
EVENING SWAYING

In the night
once more we are like the child in the womb
dreaming
or the shepherd asleep by a moonlit hill when it
is warm
with his companions the sheep and the wise leaves; or
we are
like the lovers entwined dreaming of our original unity
as we
ride on gentle waves we know not where but assured

of his and her
Genesis; every part of the body-and-soul on such a
      fortunate night
receives messages; then when leaves and flowers open to the day
      our life has something
      convincing to say.

KEATS IS WRITING HIS LETTERS

Chianti Classico!
we want the classics, we want the wine,
      Pan and the
perfection of Tuscany, hillsides by Fiesole
      and outside of
Siena; Pan slept here, Venus touched her
      nipple; Botticelli
swooned; Maenads swayed; seasons and the
      bodies of lovers
matured. It mattered to be murmuring
      love sounds, it
mattered to be classico; in this light or glass
      of perfection
friendship like grapes matured. There was Flora,
      there was
Petrarca, there was Laura, I touched your toes, there was
      breeze; we were in
the throes of ripening; the nightingale heard unseen, the
      purple stained mouth, the
      blushful Hippocrene.

THE GIFT OF ALL KINDS OF FOOD AND HOPE

This
imbibing can be biblical
      of water ! of wine !
      of air ! of words ,
and this hunger that monsters and oceans and
      scholars and scientists also

              share with me
is necessary. Makes me shake my head to think
                    that for 71 years I have eaten so much,
                    an incredible amount and am still
                    somewhat light, yesterday stomping
in our bed room to a tape of Balinese gamelan music.
                    Think of the fields of rice I have eaten !
                    the mountains of potatoes ! the
                    blessed loaves of bread ! the
thousands of chickens !! and so on—*pasta* that
I will not say *basta* to until even after I have
become fire and air and light I hope. Song I hope.
I apologize, I thank God; I hope my songs
                    will nourish others.

A PURE DESIRE ON A GLOOMY DRAB DAY

        O Polenta—
        I want something like you
                on a foggy day—
        here it is gray vague cloudy
                dreary Maine
        gettting cold November and I want
                something
        like a yellow saint, *bright*, something
                to stand me
        in good stead—like my grandparents'
                cooking for me,
        a very bright yellow warm supper, a
                bowl like a
        mother's breast to hold; yes, I want
                to be
        nourished and very happy like
                a loved child—
        O Santa Polenta, I am about
                to lift the
        spoon and eat and be saved !

VINO ROSSO, PER PIACERE

In the Beginning was the WORD—
                           some fine poets told us.
In the end—for us—we don't know,
        the hiccup, the Nursing home,
        the gas chamber, the confused flickering
        of all the TV programs ever seen ? or the
joyous thought of a happy marriage of a grandchild ? 1st and last
things are all right for some theologians, extreme fictions, some fine,
        but give me the Marriage of Cana,
        give me some wine.

I HEAR YOU, I GET YOU

    I need a catchy tune
    to catch up with my unseen but always
            present
    ancestors, humming or whistling or singing some
            phrases
    in the mountains, sometimes above the clouds, or
            in a cozy
    corner of a fine smelling kitchen, the beat, the
            mode, the
    tune of the vowel reminds us of how we belong
            to each other.

DO NO HARM TO THIS ABUNDANCE

I honestly think
                each grain of rice
                is a fit subject for God
                is worthy of a song, deserves
                religious veneration; poets with
                respect and nourishment are not at a loss
                for subjects. You've seen rice terraces going
                down to the sea, curved going up to the sky;

you've been where all the Buddhas are born, where all the
poems are made, are waiting for readers.

TO CONTINUE NOURISH PURELY OUR RESPECT

If I were to thank
appropriately and sufficiently every grain of rice
    that I have eaten
it would take all the reincarnations of my life, take
    longer than going
up and down all those wet and cloud attended
    rice territories of
China, Indonesia, Malaysia, Japan, longer than it
    would take to
thank the gods of all the mythologies East and West.
    The best
we can do is particularly be nourished, grow in our
    sense of the
sacred, be abundantly satisfied, seek to help, and
    give vigor to
Celebrations.

NOW FOR 50 YEARS WE'VE SORT OF KNOWN
EACH OTHER; OUR 41ST YEAR IN MAINE

Sloop, you slip, you slide,
    we sleep,
we stoop to conquer, we rise to
    talk and
sneeze and glide again, and again
    and again
we douse ourselves with surprise,
    bewildered
we find more boats, more voyages;
    we notice that
a breeze hails our way, we lift our
    sails; we hold
on to each other for dear life.

DO YOU KNOW YOUR SCIENCE,
DO YOU GENEROUSLY ACT OUT YOUR LIFE ?

Poem
or the dance
as some sort of aphrodisiac,
  food, drink,
for some sort of prologue, nourishment;
  sex, play,
sea motion and saxophone messages as some
  sort of
massage, temporary climax, prologue; a
  mathematician
or mystic must be dizzy, delirious,
  hopefully
delighted as he considers that in just
  one ejaculation
there are about 200 million acrobats;
  upward bound
wiggling voyagers, dancers; what is the upshot
  of all this
when you consider all the days and nights of love
  you've had
and even perhaps some lesser agitated Italians
  and even others
have surprisingly had ? You look up and see the
  Milky Way, a
small part of one separate galaxy and consider
  all the
poems, sea horses, splurgings, other galaxies
  that help
us pass the time and cooperate with music
  and Creation.

FURTIVELY AND SUBLIMINALLY AWARE
OF EACH OTHER

Wouldn't you know that the woodchuck would come out of the
  woods on a
drizzly day ? it knowing that most people are inside watching
  TV or listening to FM or

having coffee,
he or she, small, fluffy, brown reddish light, hints from
        hunger and raindrops
help forethought, he or she sidles by the bushes, going towards
        the future and patches of farm,
he or she is preparing for the future family, burrowing, furrowing,
        further into racial mythology
than Jung, slightly hesitant but persistent perpetrator frequents
        the bank of forget-me-nots; the sound
of the rain encourages us to drink our cup of coffee, to filter
        filter our respect through the
        comedy of celebration.

ON THE OCCASION OF MEETING A GREAT POEM
OR A GREAT PAINTING

One goes through hundreds of rooms where they (the paintings) and I
        have not as
exactly and as fully as possible arrived and one realizes that's natural,
        frequent, as with
people or city streets, time that does not seem like your Awakening.
        But then a Sunflower
by Blake or Van Gogh comes into or out of our lives, it grows
        wider, it has
the Unnameable as the Center and within that the sun and our solar
        system and our genesis.
We generate more fables, more bibles, after this Event. The
        vibrations in the seeds
of the prayers of the saints from everywhere and all time are
        contained in the darkness
        and time of that union.

AFTER RETURNING TO MAINE; AFTER HEARING A GOOD LECTURE BY DANIEL HOFFMAN ABOUT ROBERT FROST; AFTER REREADING "CHOOSE SOMETHING LIKE A STAR"

Better than coins,
better than proverbs, though proverbs please
      at times, and coins sometimes
      are useful,
better than theologies, though theologies tantalize and give us
      a chance of wordiness, and at times
      helpful directions;
these autumn leaves now at the end of Maine October
      that I see plentifully almost
      everywhere; a small
squirrel making its tiny waves of bounce above all
      this generosity,
nourishment for the earth, reminders of our seasons, reasons,
      colorful ancestors,
time for harvest and to begin the (endless ?) task of counting
      one's lucky stars;
bemused choose something like a Robert Frost poem; how modern we are
      as the leaves are slightly blown, as
      the amazing cycles turn and
      turn and turn.

TAKING A WOODEN STATUE OF DON QUIXOTE DOWN FROM THE TOP OF MY SCHOOL OFFICE BOOKSHELF AS I AM ABOUT TO RETIRE AND TRANSPOSE HIM TO A SECRET PLACE WE NEED HIS COURAGE, I VOW ETERNAL SUPPORT

Whatever you do
whatever is done to you
by all the materialist skeptics confused mundane
      distracted ones
of the turning world, somewhat or completely blind to what
      you see, don't
don't give up, Quixote ! where would the Golden Age go
      then, where where
would our increasing heightening nobility potency be

357

without your

dignity ? where and how did you dig the Golden Age up,
    we need to know;
go go always with the thought of the perfect Dulcinea,
    sweeten our hope,
strengthen our poetry. Don't be short changed for the
    mundane practicalities;
that's right I see you lift the lance again against
    the fickle winds of
change, against the turning windmills. There's chivalry !
    there's charity !
irrevocable one, dearest wreck, loftiest uncle, don't give up
    the Golden belief in Us.

ALL FOR THE GAZING AND AMAZING

Gazelles, deer, impala, wildebeest, water buffalo, *etc.*,
    I'm thinking of
words, words in all these great books East and West in my library
    and that they
are vital and in groups and in motion like many animals in
    the high grass
on the great plains of Africa, a life within them, a beauty
    as of zebras
in groups standing still or suddenly moving, the necessity
    of their birth,
of their form, of their get-together, of their rhythmical or
    thunderous motion,
the same life within the animals, within the words, and all
    their antecedents, relatives,
the swishing of tails, the sounds their bodies make in a
    panorama or poem, all this
    is a wonder for me.

FARE WELL, TRAVEL WELL, SAID THE RESOUNDING RITUALISTIC GONGS GONGS TO THE TRAVELLER

Gone, gone, gone,
       where have you gone, books,
       where have you gone, ancestors
       where have you gone, all those millions of words
         that excited me, Alyosha Karamazov's words and others,
         billions of snow flakes that soaked into the ground
         that always surprised me in many different countries
         of the world ? I was thinking of you, books in
my office, when I started this commencing transition thought
as I looked up from my desk and saw only a few remaining,
2 small old copies of the essays of Emerson, some grammar
books to give away to foreign students, who's not foreign ?
Transacted, transposed, hundreds already carried by hand
to my somewhat secluded studio; enamoured thoughts,
those words from Plato's Realm of Ideas,
from Radhakrishnan and *Dhammapada*,
the ongoing body of my poetry
respects you; give courage,
give strength to the
ongoing journey.

INVULNERABLE CONTINUOUS CHANT

     Down come the pictures,
    yesterday the huge long stone rubbing
         bought at a
    temple in Xian of the wandering Chinese monk
         returning from India
    with the scriptures in scrolls carried on
         his back,
    returning by foot, it took many years,
         to disciples
    waiting in China, it took many centuries
         to my office in
    Maine and yesterday (since I retired from my
         official duties)
    to my studio by a small hill. Near my

library I hope
to hear his scriptures unrolling, his and our
sutras unfolding.

TO CARE, TO CARRY, TO FIND THE CHORUS IN DIFFERENT CIRCLES OF PARADISE

By hand, by foot,
not by donkey, not by car,
but by hand and foot and body and soul
      scared, scarred,
shaken such as it is, and must be, and change,
      I carried them,
group by group, chorus by chorus of mysteries,
      my books from my office,
many of them uphill, up Mountain Avenue, to my
      little house of retirement;
all secluded with the liberal arts; shadows, pine
      trees by Mt. David;
changing light in the eastern exposure of my so
      mystic studio;
the mountain uplifts me; the books, the books,
      to name them would make
the poem very long, very religious, uphold us,
      their words like flickerings
from fish make us profound, like flames from many
      phoenixes surprise the
      transported soul.

YOUR GLANCE OR STANCE CAN CHANGE MY CUSTOMS, COSTUMES

If you want me to be
a colorful horse with spangles and plumes
and mirrors and noise

just make me one

if you want me to be
an elephant with histories
and gods like tapestries all over
my body ready to uplift you

just make me one

if you want me to be a Snake or Sun
imitating a dancer with a thousand motions
and with feet that at times imitate flowers at times fire

with your desire
just make me one

CONTRADICTING THE STATEMENT
THAT SHE STAGED HER LAST
PERFORMANCE (FOR SUKANYA)

Presented.
But they're not dead, the fires are
        still lighting
other fires, those sparks started by her
        stomping feet,
her romantic sacred gestures, warmed up
        by Krishna,
and before that enkindling flute player
        there were other
gods who set the mind-body in motion, one
        galaxy sees
another as a Kathakali dancer, the fact is
        that it flared,
fireworks in India or flute music under the
        belly of a
leaf, what can stop when once illuminated
        with such
playful necessary religious fervor ? that
        doesn't retire,
it changes its course, the seer burning is
        a holy fire,
from his hands as he turns the pages of the
        holy book more fires
        are sent forth.

PASSIONS WHICH INCLUDE
THE WORD PERHAPS MORE OFTEN

Going into retirement or exile as
        so many
of the Chinese poets did can help
        give one
some advantages of sometimes solitude,
        one talks
more often to oneself; free of official quarrels
        or demands;
these inner dialogues might lead to poetry
        or painting,
some art of reflection, contemplation, we
        hope laughter,
not exemption from some pains and worries of old age,
        a little more
detachment? detachment which is another kind
        of freedom, another
        kind of passion.

SAYING GOOD-BYE TO 2 RETIRING ASSISTANTS

In your quiet way in secluded recesses
        you have helped,
yes, I have to admit I took you for granted, you
        who kept me
somewhat fulfilled, you who adjusted so easily to
        my moving
around from one country to another, Yugoslavia, Brazil,
        China, India,
never objected to my bragging about travelling, to my
        eating so much, there
mostly in the dark you in your destined corner
        assisted, now
we must separate; I don't think you had illusions concerning
        fame and adventure,
now it is time for us, you 2 teeth way back there, to part
        company;
it will be temporarily bloody, painful, doubly holy;
        I say thank you.

Have I become
    a bit of a turkey? my skin,
    well, that's not bad—being an old
    relative to a turkey, Benjamin Franklin
    wanted him to be the American bird rather
    than the bald eagle; I trot, and I give
Thanksgiving; I gobble gobble as I did in Grammar School,
I love abundance of feathers, of poems, also I am
proud of the way Monet memorized me, depicted us,
glorious, eminent, presidential, presiding over
backyard food, aware of gabbing; also I think of the
grand exotic country I visited once whose name is
related to this monumental bird; I remember pashas
imitating it in their ample robes and harems;
I recall whirling dervishes in Konya;
be a thankful turkey with me.

THE SPORTIVE LIFE AS A MORAL VICTORY AND/OR SOME FIND IT DIFFICULT TO TACKLE THE NAME TAGLIABUE (FOR COUSIN PAUL TAGLIABUE, COMMISSIONER OF THE NFL)

Something to tackle,
something to take on,
something to tag on, here are poems to tag on to
    all the football players
in the world, number them so competition and aggression
    become a touching
and tackling and tumbling and tossing and topsy turvy
    sport—
energetic, hustling, huffing, crouching, running, grabbing,
    one gets on top of
another and others pile on to make a momentary mountain
    of costumed beefy men
accustomed to tackling; helmeted like Greek warriors, broad shouldered,
    some heavy and rampaging,
these vigorous players in snow and rain or brilliant sun and wind
    in Fall and Winter
sometimes tremendously fall and quickly rise and shine. Sometimes

battered and boisterous
they kick, they run, they catch. Audiences wildly applaud,
    we all win when we turn
    wars into exuberance
    of Sports.

AND BREEZE BY THE ARAB CAFÉS, AT NIGHT

Incomparable civilization
in certain tones of voice
in certain tones of colors—
which ones are strongest for you? for me
Cézanne, Monet, many others; who knows
        how it is
achieved—the civilization, at times the
        incomparable
and in worldly terms heaven. A soprano sings
        and the high fountain
of some unseen and flower scented Alhambra
        rises, rises,
a tone poem by Ravel gains in voluptuousness,
        a sound, a sequence
of ecstasy quietly conveying sound of a guitar,
        shadows with the scent
of jasmine; my memory returns to my young days by
        the Lebanese sea in its
time of peace, green, light blue, lavender; cool,
        Sufi sufficient,
        luxurious.

WITHIN THE CONSTRUCTED WONDER
WE ARE AROUSED TO FURTHER
UNFATHOMABLE CONTINUITY

Who needs it, the poem ?
who needs the blind beggar around
        the corner
chanting the Koran ? we instinctively

                    grope like the
        Magi, like the child at the breast, like
                    Hercules
        not sure of what he wants but urgent
                    exercising
        his expendable vigor by sumptuous Venus
                    or musical Venice;
        need, need, necessitates the dreamers to baffled
                    make the Taj Mahal.

THE INTUITION AND INSISTENCE OF SURVIVORS

        How many woodpeckers have I been and for
                    how
        many years, I'm not thinking of sex but
                    obviously I am too,
        I'm thinking of the sound I've made it seems for centuries
                    hitting the typewriter keys,
        Paderewski at the piano couldn't have been more
                    loyal, royal, kept
        in more musical practice procedure than I;
                    we strike our notes,
        we note that somewhere somewhere we think you
                    are in need of listening;
        you dress your best, you address your best, to
                    go to the concert;
        the compelled one at the keyboard keeps stirring
                    the alphabet into action,
        print, prayer, daring hopes; the beating of the
                    heart, the coursing of the
        messages, the persistency of those famished feathered woodpeckers,
                    the fame of the secrecy of love,
                    make timely necessity,
                    make strength apparent.

PRESCIENCE

There are
map makers
and there are astrologers
and there are people seeing various reflections
of their changing
selves in the reflection of the long window as
they look at the
changing colors of the light of the wide sky; it
so happens that
not wanting to feel lost or thoughtless I must
so often contrive
the moment, whatever I see, the delicate tips fanning out
of the slender February
trees, the curve of the tops of these trees, these fine
tributaries; what do
I attribute to you that's in this or that moment of seeing?
desire to blossom
before you.

NON-POSSESSIVE I RETURNED TO THE POEM

He or she
allowed me to approach very closely
as if
it were a painting or a person,
it was
in tall fine profile like my mother
at her
thinnest aristocratic and well dressed,
it had
feathers, the whole high upstanding body
seemed to
eye me, I to I, spirit to spirit,
the blue
heron and I perceived each other,
our seeing
gave our souls away; non-possessive
it returned to
the sky.

SEEN LATER FINALLY BY
A TRANSFORMED PERSON

Each inevitable poem a dance gesture, a cadence of a
          necessary motion,
a musical untranslatable notion, a meteor's message
          in the mouth of a fish,
a flame that travels on the sea like quick reflections, on
          the land from country to country,
a whispering of disciples before the resurrection, a clue for
          all migrations, flocks
of shadows over highest lakes; I like you, I need you,
          the most personal poem said
to someone unknown everywhere; I knew you in our previous
          lives; when we were side
by side in Abraham's bosom, like prophetic blade of grass
          near its kindred green soul;
flamenco or future dance; sometimes accompanied by crickets
          or castanets; I started to say
each inevitable turn, gesture, part of a long drawn out
          inevitable saraband.

I WHISPER THIS TO YOU, BARTERED ONE

Correspondent
philosophic correspondent
desiring and responsive correspondent,
I want to send you a letter or ten thousand
          poems,
where are you? if it is too many for you it is not
          too many for me;
you? is it what we call God since we *need* a
          name for the Nameless
the distant the nearest the unseen? then I know
          all desire and all poems
are not too many for you any more than they are
          for me, where am I?
let us say that atman is the brahman, that the
          Oversoul is particular
and see how Emerson helps out. We read him and others
          that we correspond with

know that fulfillment is immeasurable, and though we want
        to address the letter
we know the receiver and response is anyone who is everywhere.

SLIDING INTO THE FUTURE

Achieving?
what is there to achieve? the event occurs at its
        own accord
as the sea shell is made or the volcano erupts
        or the lines
of a Shakespeare play are memorized; in due time
        It Happens
momentously temporarily, the snow cap melts,
        the sea anemone
blossoms, the lizard's shadow is sketched in the
        memory.
The anguish in the sick bed is engraved on
        the foam.
Forms keep changing; clouds as much as deities;
        and Zeus
is bewildered, transformed. The opulent is found
        or lost in
the twinkling of an eye. Someone performs a
        ritual in shadows.
The lover leaves his bed; none knows what will
        happen next.
Achievements flare up like the flames of orange moths
        on Paros.
Faces keep appearing from the distant past. Boats appear
        with cargoes never seen before.

NON-POSSESSIVE GENEROSITY GENERATIONS

I could say superficially what they are right away
        and you
might superficially understand, you will guess before long,
        they are

not germs or viruses or gazelles or elephants or parades
        of costumed people,
but like animals like vines like thoughts concerning the
        divine like
urges motions waves molecular action galaxies in a
        dervish they
are vital active and gods I keep releasing them, have to,
        no matter
whether a reader asks for them or an editor is commercially
        concerned
they which are forms of speech are the marks of prayer are
        the footwork of dancers
words words you said it keep emerging like seeds like
        sea horses from the emission of the sea
like assistants to testaments they keep emerging as diviners
        out of a space ship
keep coming from my life my body which has no
        beginning nor end.

ACTUALLY HELPING

No doubt in unique and countless ways
        we are foolish
but we can in our slight and wondrous
        ways relate
to the gods, for instance the light of the
        early morning sun
which enters my studio, casts its brightness
        on the wall, illuminates
my postcard of ancient bearded Camillo Pissarro,
        and my scene of Florence rooftops with
Santa Maria del Fiore at the center. Temporarily
        I can make my shadow
move on the wall. I can help my spirit write
        old fashioned words—like
        gods, saint, wonder.

ALL ABSOLUTE ATTENTION

She
did not know she was reading between the words, the lines,
      when
an angel unknowingly desired swept into the room, it
      was
an annunciation the adventure of which brought in all
      light.
All things became the gathered Word once more. She trembled,
      bowed
to It; matured the Godhead into this world; a child, a
      suffering
person, a generosity beyond all measure, all comprehension.
      Wise men
began their journeys, offered whatever gifts they had, found themselves
      Saved.

THE PURPOSE THAT CAN BE NAMED
IS NOT THE PURPOSE

For whatever it's worth a fish must go its course;
      whatever
gets into its head gives it a determined headstrong
      direction
so salmon and Solomon go up the stream; why ? why ? the
      philosopher not wet
asks; but Solomon in his trance and dance and the silver
      salmon in its
o'erleaping purposes, struggling and spawning sufficiently,
      splatter us
at least slightly with their necessity and light. The
      directions of a
star begotten in the womb wish us forward. Onward.
      The bewildered
philosopher scratches his head; volumes will appear forever
      about teleology
and theology. God Himself at Cana in a trance in a dance
      gives out the wine generously.
      We are intoxicated
      With Purpose.

"NOW IN A MOMENT I KNOW
WHAT I AM FOR, I AWAKE."

The poem awakes in every moment of its utterance
    and never ends,
it is what the sea gull unseen does to the air about us,
    curved,
what the curled and wet uprisen air announces, moved
    by ocean and
moon; light of the full huge bright moon seen in the
    darkness
before the day of our labors. Labors if known as rituals
    as
services to God are parts of the continued prayer.

FOR SOME OF JEROME ROBBINS' THOUGHTS
CONCERNING BACH'S GOLDBERG VARIATIONS

Are those gestures
    written on the waters of the world ?
    the mind, where is it, the memory
where is it ? those graceful varied diversified unified
    fluent it seems almost supernatural
    curves of the arms, motions of
the hands, leaps of the beautiful bodies, very young,
    fluent and remind us of respect, play, ardor,
emotions of freedom from the pressures of the will,
    reminding us of thoughts that make flowers
    blossom, petals in the softness and
celebration, Bach in his ascendancy, ease, perfections and
    delight, a place of no graves, a source
    of beginnings in Eden, the seed of
innocence, songs that bodies make to remind us of
    angels, diversity in light's music,
    the many in the One.

NOT HELD CAPTIVE BY PENCIL,
HOUSE, OR TRAVEL BAG

Do not feel unsteady, but you do not really possess me,
    said the chair;
do not worry, said the table, you can write sitting or
    standing without me,
you do not really possess me; and the light bulb and
    lamp shade
reminded me I didn't, though I could be enlightened
    with humor and
knew it was free of me; hate and attachments are forms of
    possessions and
I did not hate them or really need them; I possessed
    only my life;
    I was free.

THE PAST THAT IS VITAL IS ALREADY HERE
AND IN THE FUTURE

Don't look back, Orpheus, or
    she will
disappear; before you both leave
    tell each other
don't dwell on the past of what you
    and the world
were, see what is at your feet, hear
    the sound you
make in the moment, notice the light
    in all objects,
life ahead of you like countless proclamations
    of leaves,
    of stars.

Light
plays upon our feelings as if
we were the body of a violin   it's
          quite something !
what can happen to the body and its spirit
          and its
lyricism and response when touched upon by
          breeze or
storm or by piano music or by the
          touch or
even the glance of a person. Birds and all
          creatures, the
earth itself, are aroused, responsive, to the
          coming of dawn
which first stirred these words that were
          asleep. Each
vital object in the world, worm, bee, tree,
          has its
melody. Light changes, the soil or soul of
          expression
changes, the energy, thought, from ourselves,
          fingertips
or sight or sex changes, tones are innumerable;
          darkness
too is as sacred, productive, varied, creative
          as light.

JUST IN TIME TO NOTICE

Tiniest
fragile microscopic delicate
spider wiggling in our house the day before
          Christmas,
maker of patterns, bridge builder, acrobat in
          complete
cosmic space, like Marcel Marceau or Chaplin in
          a silent movie
looking at you. Think of that ! that we were born
          to be involved

in the same pantomime. Now you, reader, make a
        jest, a gesture.

DESCENDANTS AND SUNS GIVE US
A CERTAIN PERSPECTIVE

We stop for a moment to
        collect the sun
into our bodies; so familiar fire
        can converse
with familiar fire; something is always
        happening to
energy and time and we are in the fields or
        we are on the
mountains or we are looking at an illuminated
        manuscript,
suddenly out of the blades of grass came
        saints dancing.

EXCHANGE AND ECSTASY

Now if you need a word for the Nameless you must
        include
every letter, every word, in the dictionary and include
        the word
Nameless. You must even see your name involved.
        Write it large,
write it small, it doesn't matter, it is not erasable
        and whatever
the Nameless is with all of its names involved it demands
        its and their
coming into existence. All those unique sounds spoken on
        the Sahara
or Mesopotamia or on a cliff in Colorado or in a cool
        chapel in Italy
or the Baptistry of Pisa. Specific. Pure. Unique.
        Unquenchable.
It comes and holds every chalice. It touches the coins

that make the
spirit fabulous. Fables emerge from it like fireflies in
        the night or like
sounds in all the songs by the Nile or Benares or wherever there is
        the need for the Other.

THE COLLECTED POEM

I didn't want it to be
                an entertainment commodity
                a seminar commodity
                an attitude to be approved of
                by this fashion or that ideology

I had no plans or programs or theories for it
                but it was from my heart
                of no importance
                of all importance
        it was not to be named or foretold
        it alone gave me freedom

ONE OF THE MANY MAGIC BRANCHES

Not all branches can break into buds
        all times of the year
but there is the magic branch poetry that
        when there are the
occasions of seeing a friend, of wanting one, of
        saying welcome or
farewell, such occasions recognized as mystical,
        since there are souls in things,
then the book you are holding, magical reader, becomes a
        light long branch with
        many flowers.

Index of TITLES and First Lines